DFJSM

Function Modelling

Office of Government Commerce

D1421992

London: TSO

Published by TSO (The Stationery Office) and available from:

Online
www.tso.co.uk/bookshop

Mail, Telephone, Fax & E-mail
TSO
PO Box 29, Norwich NR3 1GN
Telephone orders/General enquiries 0870 600 5522
Fax orders: 0870 600 5533
Email: book.orders@tso.co.uk
Textphone: 0870 240 3701

TSO Shops
123 Kingsway, London WC2B 6PQ
020 7242 6393 Fax 020 7242 6394
68-69 Bull Street, Birmingham B4 6AD
0121 236 9696 Fax 0121 236 9699
9-21 Princess Street, Manchester M60 8AS
0161 834 7201 Fax 0161 833 0634
16 Arthur Street, Belfast BT1 4GD
028 9023 8451 Fax 028 9023 5401
18-19 High Street, Cardiff CF10 1PT
029 2039 5548 Fax 029 2038 4347
71 Lothian Road, Edinburgh EH3 9AZ
0870 606 5566 Fax 0870 606 5588

TSO Accredited Agents
(See Yellow Pages)

and through good booksellers

For further information on OGC products, contact:

OGC Service Desk
Rosebery Court
St Andrews Business Park
Norwich NR7 0HS
Telephone + 44 (0) 845 000 4999

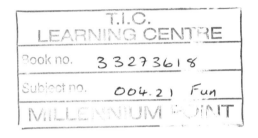

Published for the Office of Government Commerce under licence from the Controller of Her Majesty's Stationery Office.

First published 2000
Second impression 2004

ISBN 0 11 330875 2

The OGC is now the authority for best practice in commercial activities in UK Government, combining a number of separate functions with related aims.

OGC will build on the popular guidance developed by the former CCTA and others, working with organisations internationally to develop and share business and practitioner guidance within a world-class best practice framework.

Titles within the Business Systems Development series include:

SSADM Foundation	ISBN 0 11 330870 1
Data Modelling	ISBN 0 11 330871 X
The Business Context	ISBN 0 11 330872 8
User-Centred Design	ISBN 0 11 330873 6
Behaviour and Process Modelling	ISBN 0 11 330874 4
Function Modelling	ISBN 0 11 330875 2
Database and Physical Process Design	ISBN 0 11 330876 0
Also available as a boxed set	ISBN 0 11 330883 3

Printed in the United Kingdom for The Stationery Office
Id 164273 C3 02/04 932886 19585

CONTENTS

FOREWORD

The Business Systems Development (BSD) series represents 'best practice' approaches to investigating, modelling and specifying Information Systems. The techniques described within this series have been used on systems development projects for a number of years and a substantial amount of experience has contributed to the development of this guidance.

Within the BSD series the techniques are organised into groups that cover specific areas of the development process, for example *User Centred Design* which covers all aspects of the investigation, specification and design of the user interface.

The techniques provide a practical approach to the analysis and design of IT systems. They can also be used in conjunction with other complementary techniques such as Object-Oriented techniques.

The material used within this series originated in the Structured Systems Analysis and Design Method (SSADM) which was introduced by the CCTA as a standard method for the development of medium to large IT systems. Since its introduction in the early 1980's, SSADM has been developed through a number of versions to keep pace with the evolving technology and approaches in the IT industry.

The *SSADM Foundation* volume within the BSD series describes the basic concepts of the method and the way in which it can be employed on projects. It also describes how the different techniques can be used in combination. Each of the other volumes in the series describes techniques and approaches for developing elements of the overall specification and design. These can be used in conjunction with one another or as part of alternative approaches. Cross-referencing is provided in outline within the description of each of the techniques to give pointers to the other approaches and techniques that should be considered for use in combination with the one being described.

All volumes within the Business System Development series are available from:

The Stationery Office
St Crispins
Duke Street
Norwich
NR3 1PD

Acknowledgments

Laurence Slater of Slater Consulting Ltd is acknowledged for editing existing material and where necessary developing new material for the volumes within the Business Systems Development series. John Hall, Jennifer Stapleton, Caroline Slater and Ian Clowes are acknowledged for much of the original material on which this series is based.

The following are thanked for their contribution and co-operation in the development of this series:

Paul Turner	-	Parity Training
Tony Jenkins	-	Parity Training
Caroline Slater	-	Slater Consulting Ltd

In addition to those named above a number of people agreed to review aspects of the series and they are thanked accordingly.

1   INTRODUCTION

This volume in the *Business Systems Development* series is concerned with the analysis of processing and data within the system and the definition of the required system processing (Data Flow Modelling) and off-line functions (Function Definition).

With Data Flow Modelling the analyst can document the way in which data is processed in any current system and demonstrate the way it will be processed in the system that is to be developed. Once that has been completed the analyst can then use the data flow model to help identify those units of processing (known as functions) which will be developed. Although Data Flow Modelling will assist the user in identification of all functions, within this manual only the derivation of off-line functions will be covered (i.e., those functions which require no user intervention). On-line functions (those that contain some element of user interaction) are covered by *User Centred Design* in this series.

The use of Data Flow Modelling will assist the analyst in a number of ways:

- to clearly identify and document the scope of the new system;

- to document the way in which the processing elements of the system transform data entering the system into data which is output from and stored within the system. This can include both the system that is to be developed and also any existing system;

- to demonstrate to the users of the system that the analyst has a grasp of what the system is required to do and what any current system does.

The use of Function Definition is fundamental to the development of the new system in that it defines the individual units of processing that will be carried forward to design and development of the new system. In addition, Function Definition;

- helps to pull together the different analysis and design products;

- helps in the planning of the development of the new system;

- provides a basis for the sizing of the new system.

In this series all products are shown in the context of the System Development Template (SDT). This is a template which divides the system development process into areas of concern onto which the development products can be mapped. Annexe A provides a fuller description of the System Development Template. Figure 1-1 shows how the products of Function Modelling fit into the System Development Template.

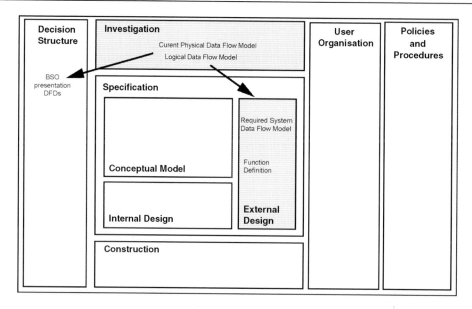

Figure 1-1 Place of Function Modelling products in the System Development Template

Organisation of this manual

After this (introductory) chapter, the volume is organised as follows.

Chapter 2 – Data Flow Modelling. This is a full description of the concepts, products and techniques necessary for the development of Data Flow Models.

Chapter 3 – Function Definition. This is a full description of the concepts, products and techniques necessary for the identification and documentation of functions.

Chapter 4 – Meta-model. To assist those working on the projects to understand the relationship between the concepts used within this volume a meta-model is provided which shows the basic concepts covered in this volume and way they inter-relate.

Chapter 5 – Product Descriptions. Product descriptions are provided for all the major products described in this volume. These should be used by projects as a basis for the product descriptions to be used on the project. (Note: It is expected that the project will need to tailor these product descriptions so that items not required are omitted and any other items required by the project included.)

Annexes. There are three annexes appended to this manual. The first gives a description of the System Development Template, the second is a description of EU-Rent which is the case study that is used throughout this manual. The third is a glossary of terms that are relevant to this manual.

2   DATA FLOW MODELLING

Data Flow Modelling is used to investigate the flow of data around a system:

- to and from agents external to the system;

- to and from processes which transform the data;

- into and out of repositories or stores of data;

- to act as the basis of subsequent design.

The technique can be used to model a physical system or a logical abstraction of that system.

Data Flow Modelling is used within several different parts of the System Development Template (see Figure 2-1):

- **Investigation** where the technique is used to model the current system as it is actually implemented and derive a logical view of the current system;

- **Decision Structure** where the technique can be used, if appropriate, to present alternative designs for the new system, each of which satisfies the requirements for the system;

- **Specification** where the technique is used as the first part of External Design to develop a clear picture of the required system.

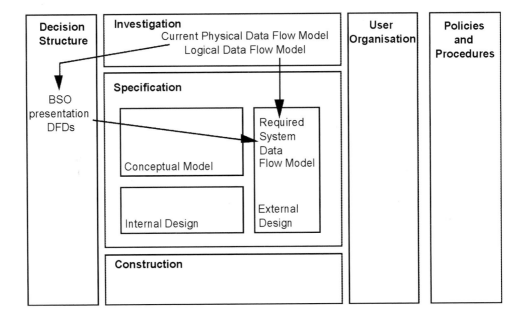

Figure 2-1 Data Flow Modelling in the System Development Template

Data Flow Modelling has several main purposes:

- to identify and clearly define the scope and boundary of the system and its various components;

- to identify requirements for the new system;

- to help in the identification of events and functions;

- to assist in communications between analyst and user.

Three different Data Flow Models can be produced during a development project. These are:

- **Current Physical Data Flow Model**, which represents the existing system as it is currently implemented;

- **Logical Data Flow Model**, which represents the current system without any physical constraints;

- **Required System Data Flow Model**, which represents a logical view of the new system without any physical constraints and structured around the user's view of the system.

It is the last of these models (Required System Data Flow Model) which is considered the most important in that it represents a view of the system that will be developed and, as such, will provide a basis for the identification and development of other analysis and design products (e.g., functions and events). The first two models, which are both a view of any existing system, are of use where there is a requirement for the new system to be similar to an existing one (either automated or manual). This is most likely where the system's operation is covered by law or where the business processes are defined and unchangeable.

Data Flow Modelling and business activities

Business Activity Modelling (covered *The Business Context* volume in this series) influences the application of Data Flow Modelling in a number of ways. The influences are summarised in Figure 2-2.

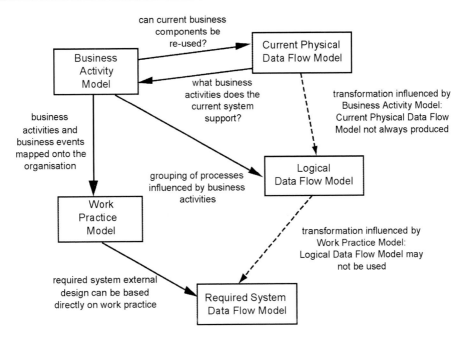

Figure 2-2 Influence of Business Activity Model and Work Practice Model on Data Flow Models

Business Activity Modelling provides a more systematic approach than the development of the Current Physical and Logical Data Flow Models to investigating the possibilities of reuse of parts of existing systems. It investigates the business requirements and can be used to evaluate the Current Physical Data Flow Model, asking the question "is what we are doing now adequate to support the business need?". If a computer system already exists, existing code may be reusable. At least, components of the code could be considered for use. Even where existing code and procedures cannot be reused, specifications may be reusable.

The analyst is required to take an objective view of the underlying data and processes during logicalisation. The development of a Business Activity Model approaches the system from an entirely different viewpoint and allows the analyst to model the essential activities of the system without becoming too involved in the detail of what is actually going on. These two different views are both very useful and can be used to complement one another in the investigation of the system.

The use of a Business Activity Model may modify the way in which the Current Physical and Logical Data Flow Models are used within a project and may even negate the benefits of developing them. There is no requirement to transform the Logical Data Flow Model into the Required System Data Flow Model. Instead, the Required System Data Flow Model can be based upon the Work Practice Model, which is the mapping of the Business Activity Model onto the user organisation.

2.1   The Concepts of Data Flow Modelling

Data Flow Models are diagrams which are made up of a number of different types of symbols. The basic types of symbols are shown below and are further explained in the subsequent paragraphs.

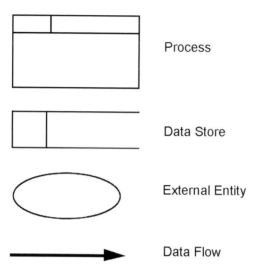

Process

Data Store

External Entity

Data Flow

Figure 2-3 Basic symbols on Data Flow Diagrams

2.1.1 Process

A process transforms or manipulates data in a system. It contains three parts (shown in Figure 2-4):

- process identifier – a unique identifier which is a number, allocated arbitrarily with no implication for priority or sequence;

- process name – the description of the process which is a simple imperative sentence, with the verb as specific as possible, e.g., 'Control Car Movements', 'Make Booking' (vague terms, such as 'process' and 'do', should be avoided);

- location/role name – this is used in the Current Physical Data Flow Diagrams only and represents the part of the organisation where the process is carried out, possibly qualified by the role of the particular part of the organisation. Role names are enclosed in square brackets.

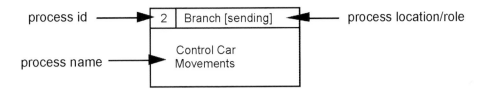

Figure 2-4 Components of a Data Flow Diagram Process

Each process on a Data Flow Diagram may be broken down into another lower level diagram of several processes if required. Each process on the decomposed diagram can be further decomposed until the desired level of detail has been reached. Where a process is decomposed, the identifiers of the lower level processes are prefixed by the identifier of the parent process. The lower-level processes are enclosed inside a frame which is the same shape as a process box and which contains the process identifier and process name of the parent process along the top. Processes which are not further decomposed are annotated with an asterisk in the bottom right corner. It is possible to have a mixture of decomposed and bottom-level processes on the same Data Flow Diagram. Process decomposition is represented in the illustration in Figure 2-5.

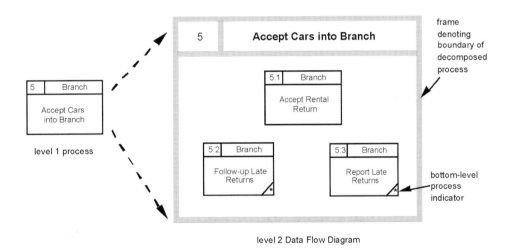

Figure 2-5 Decomposition of Data Flow Diagram process

This technique of decomposition of processes into lower level ones can prove very useful to the analyst who can develop diagrams that represent different levels of decomposition of the system. However, it is very easy to get carried away and simply keep decomposing the processes into further diagrams. This can make the model very difficult to read and understand. Therefore the analyst should exercise care when decomposing Data Flow Diagrams. As a rule of thumb three levels of decomposition (in addition to the top level) should be adequate for most systems. When decomposing a process it is generally thought that all the processes for a level should appear on the same page and that, as a broad guide, one level should contain between three and seven processes. If a process decomposes into only 2 processes then consideration should be made to including both of them at the higher level.

2.1.2 Data Store

A data store represents a repository of data inside the system boundary. If there is a current system, the data store represents a physical repository of data: a computer file or a manual means of storing data, a box file or card index, for instance. On both Logical and Required System Data Flow Diagrams data stores have no suggestion of the physical means of storage, but on the Required System Data Flow Model they will probably be implemented in the form of a computer database.

A data store is represented by an open-ended box containing the following:

- data store identifier (upper-case letter followed by a number);

- data store name – text describing the contents of the data store.

The same data store may be drawn several times on a Data Flow Diagram, to increase readability. Where a data store appears more than once on the same diagram the replication is indicated by a double vertical bar at the left-hand edge, as shown in Figure 2-6.

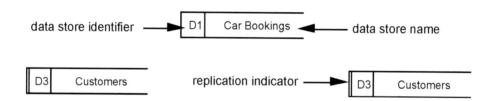

Figure 2-6 Replication of a Data Store on a Diagram

The convention for data store replication means "there is a single data store, but it has been drawn in more than one place to make the diagram easier to read". It is also possible, when modelling current physical systems, that there are multiple data stores of the same type, and more than one has to be shown on a diagram. For example, in EU-Rent's current system each branch has its own bookings file; a one-way rental requires a booking record at the pick-up branch and a record at the drop-off branch giving the expected date and time of drop-off. Role names in square brackets are used to distinguish different instances of a data store, as illustrated in Figure 2-7.

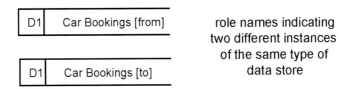

Figure 2-7 Multiple Instances of a Data Store denoted by roles

Each Data Store can be classified as follows:

- main or transient;

- physical or logical.

The different types of data store are denoted by the letter preceding the number in the data store identifier as shown in Figure 2-8.

MAIN DATA STORES

D3	Customers	Logical
D3	Customer File	Physical* (computer)
M3	Customer Register	Physical* (manual)

TRANSIENT DATA STORES

T3	Customers for today's rentals	Logical
T3	Customers transaction file	Physical* (computer)
T3 (M)	Customer Day Book	Physical* (manual)

* NB: Physical Data Stores are only permitted on Current Physical Data Flow Diagrams

Figure 2-8 Types of Data Store

Main data stores represent the data that is held centrally in a system so that it can be used by a number of different processes. Each main data store on the Data Flow Diagram has a reference letter 'D' or 'M' and an arbitrary number. 'D' indicates a computer system data store on the Current Physical Data Flow Diagrams, or any data store of the Logical or Required System Data Flow Model. 'M' indicates a clerical data store and is used only in the Current Physical Data Flow Model.

A transient data store holds data temporarily before it is used by a process and is then deleted. Transient data stores are distinguished by their identifiers being prefixed with 'T'. In Current Physical Data Flow Diagrams, the transient data store identifier may be suffixed with a 'M' to denote that the transient store is manual, not computer-based. The identifier of a manual transient data store would be, for example, 'T1(M)'. The data store contained within a process boundary may be main or transient. Transient data stores have these characteristics:

- each 'read' from a transient data store actually removes the data from the store. In other words, a data flow exiting a transient data store may be considered to be deleting that data from the data store. It follows that transient data can only be used once. If there is a requirement to read data more than once, then it must be considered to be a main data store;

- although a number of processes can add data to a transient data store, it is most probable that a single process will extract data from it;

- once data has been added to a transient data store, it cannot be updated by that process.

Data stores can be decomposed hierarchically in the same way as processes when diagrams become cluttered. Different data stores that are holding similar information can be grouped under a single data store at higher levels of the Data Flow Diagram hierarchy. The grouped data store will have a conventional data store identifier (e.g., D1) and the individual data stores that are decompositions of higher level data stores will have an alphabetic suffix added to the identifier at the lower levels (e.g., D1a, D1b). This is demonstrated in Figure 2-9.

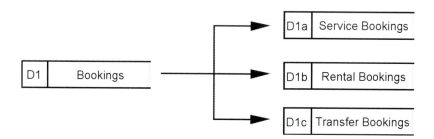

Figure 2-9 Decomposition of Data Stores

If a data store is used by only one process, it is said to be internal to that process. To avoid cluttering the Data Flow Diagram which contains the process, the internal data store is not shown. Instead, it is reflected on the Data Flow Diagram which is a decomposition of the process, inside the frame which encloses the process. Internal data stores have an identifier which includes the process identifier of the owning process, for example, D2/1, belonging to process 2 and is found only in the Data Flow Diagram that decomposes that process. At lower levels data store D2.4/1 belongs to process 2.4 only, and so on. This is shown in Figure 2-10.

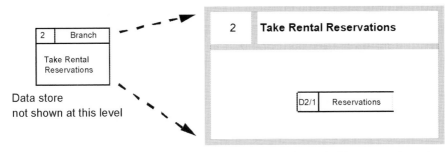

Figure 2-10 Representation of internal or local data store

2.1.3 External Entity

An external entity is a source or recipient (or both) of data in the system, and exists outside the boundary of the system. It may be a user of the system, a person or organisation outside the system, or another system. An oval symbol, completed with a meaningful name, represents the external entity. A lower-case alphabetic character is used as the external entity identifier. External entity names can be qualified by a role name enclosed in square brackets to show the role that is being adopted by the external entity. To avoid crossing data flow lines in diagrams, external entities may appear more than once on a Data Flow Diagram; replicated external entities are indicated by a diagonal line in the upper left of the oval. This is demonstrated in Figure 2-11. Where there is a large number of external entities, identifiers may extend to two alphabetic characters: aa, ab and so on.

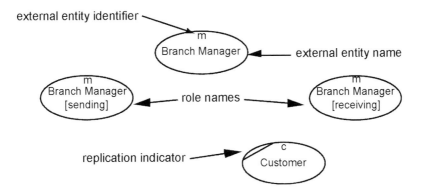

Figure 2-11 External entities

External entities may be decomposed in a similar way to data stores. The external entity identifier is extended to include a number to denote decomposed external entities. This is demonstrated in Figure 2-12.

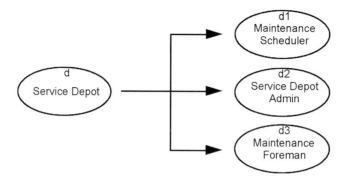

Figure 2-12 Decomposition of external entities

2.1.4 Data Flow

A data flow is represented by an arrow, with an arrowhead showing the direction of flow. Each data flow is given a name describing its contents. In some cases it is obvious what data is involved, and it is not essential to name the flow. In describing an existing system actual document titles or references may be used on Current Physical Data Flow Diagrams.

A data flow can be between a process and one of the following:

- data store;
- external entity;
- another process.

Data flows are hierarchical in line with the decomposition of the processes to which they are connected. For example, if a single data flow connects two level-1 processes, it may be split into several flows between the processes on the level 2 Data Flow Diagram. This concept is demonstrated in Figure 2-13 which shows the decomposition of a flow between an external entity and a process.

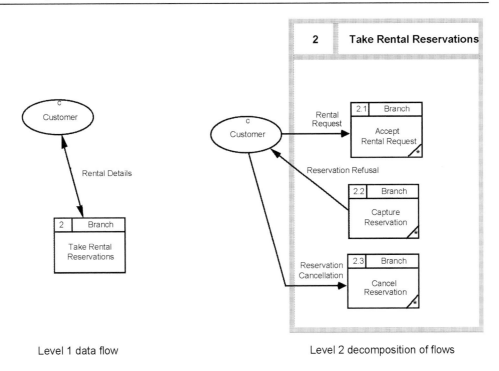

Level 1 data flow   Level 2 decomposition of flows

Figure 2-13 Decomposition of data flows

A double-headed data flow may be used on a high level Data Flow Diagram to indicate that both input and output flows appear at a lower level. At the bottom level of decomposition, all flows are one-way only.

2.2   Products of Data Flow Modelling

The main product of Data Flow Modelling is the Data Flow Model. The Data Flow Model is composed of four products:

- Data Flow Diagrams – Level 1 and Lower Levels;

- Elementary Process Descriptions;

- I/O Descriptions;

- External Entity Descriptions.

The Product Breakdown Structure for the Data Flow Model is shown in Figure 2-14.

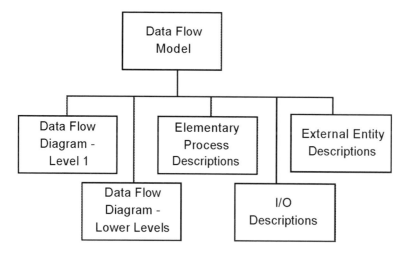

Figure 2-14 Product Breakdown Structure for Data Flow Model

There are three variants of the Data Flow Model:

- **Current Physical Data Flow Model,** which represents the existing system as it is currently implemented;

- **Logical Data Flow Model,** which represents the current system without any physical constraints;

- **Required System Data Flow Model,** which represents the new system without any physical constraints but structured around the user's view of the system.

In addition to the products covered by these three variants of the Data Flow Model, there are a number of products covered by the Data Flow Modelling technique, each of which falls into one of the following categories:

- intermediate products which are developed as an input to the Data Flow Model and are then usually discarded (Resource Flow Diagram, Document Flow Diagram, Process/Entity Matrix, Logical/Physical Data Store Cross-reference);

- products developed to cross-reference the Data Flow Model with other products (Logical Data Store/Entity Cross-reference);

- products which can use the Data Flow Modelling notations to fulfil a specific need within the project (Overview Data Flow Diagram, Data Flow Diagrams included in Business System Options, Context Diagram).

Products in the first category can be considered as being part of the practice of the technique and are therefore described in detail in this section. The Overview Data Flow Diagram and Business Systems Options Data Flow Diagrams follow the same conventions as the other Data Flow Diagrams so will not be described separately.

The dependencies between all the products mentioned above are shown in Figure 2-15. The dependencies shown on this diagram are the most common dependencies and should not be taken to be mandatory. For example, where a Business Activity Model is developed, there may be no need to develop a Current Physical Data Flow Model, in which case the main input to the Logical Data Flow Model will be the Business Activity Model. Where there is no current system, the Business Activity Model will feed directly into the Required System Data Flow Model.

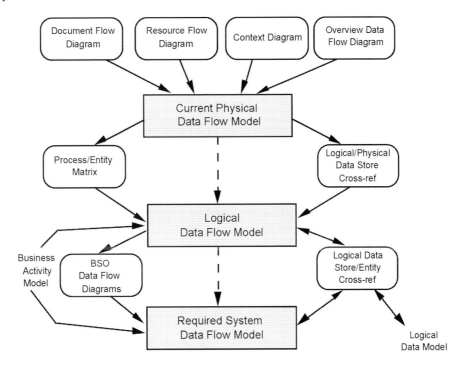

Figure 2-15 Data Flow Modelling Products

Each of the Data Flow Modelling products shown above as shaded boxes is described in more detail in this chapter. The components of the different Data Flow Models are described together as they have substantially common properties.

2.2.1 *Data Flow Diagrams (DFDs)*

A set of Data Flow Diagrams comprises a Level 1 Data Flow Diagram and Lower Level Diagrams forming a hierarchy to two or three lower levels. A Level 1 Data Flow Diagram represents the whole system on one diagram. Areas of the Level 1 Data Flow Diagram are decomposed to show successively more detail in the lower level Data Flow Diagrams.

Data Flow Diagrams should be consistent at different levels. Each lower level data flow should be represented at the next higher level as either a complete single flow or as part of a single flow:

- all objects shown communicating with a process at the higher level must be shown around the outside of the frame at the lower level;

- the sum of all the data flows crossing the frame at the lower level should match the data flows shown to and from the process at the higher level.

This is demonstrated in Figure 2-16.

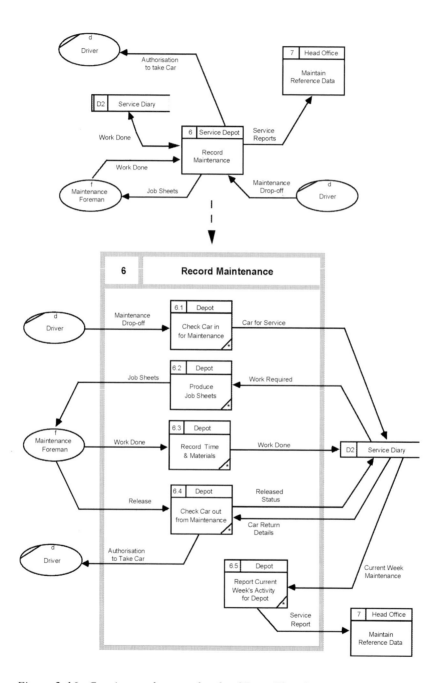

Figure 2-16   Consistency between levels of Data Flow Diagram

Maintaining consistency between different levels can result in crowded high-level Data Flow Diagrams, with many data flows that are required only for detail of error and exception handling. When Data Flow Diagrams are used for presentation, it is often helpful to omit this detail at the higher levels and only show it on the lower level diagrams.

It may also be useful to show information flows between external entities, in which case they are indicated with a dashed line, as shown in Figure 2-17.

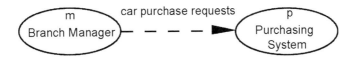

Figure 2-17 External to external flow

2.2.2 Elementary Process Descriptions

Each process at the lowest level of decomposition (i.e., which is indicated by an asterisk as being at the bottom level) is described by an Elementary Process Description (EPD).

An Elementary Process Description is a brief textual description of the process. This description may contain the following:

- what business constraints dictate how the process is carried out;

- circumstances under which the process is invoked;

- constraints on when and by whom the process can be invoked;

- what data is accessed.

Processing that is common to more than one bottom-level process is described once by a (Common) Elementary Process Description which is cross-referenced to the relevant processes. Common processes are not shown on the Data Flow Diagrams.

Figure 2-18 gives an example of two Elementary Process Descriptions. It should be stressed that this is only an example, the format being dependent upon the tools available to the project.

Id	Process Name	Description
1.1	Write Off Car	Record write-off for car. If car was booked for rental a notification will be produced automatically for rebooking another car. If car was booked for transfer or maintenance, cancel the booking and phone or fax receiving branch/service depot.
1.2	Sell Car	Check whether car to be sold is booked for rental or transfer; if it is, sale transaction cannot proceed. Sale transaction will remove car from cars available for rent or transfer; it can then be physically sold. If it was booked for maintenance, phone or fax the depot to cancel.

Figure 2-18 Elementary Process Description

2.2.3 External Entity Descriptions

A description is created for each external entity. The analyst records here any relevant detail about the external entity and possible constraints on how it interfaces or is required to interface to the system.

Figure 2-19 gives an example of an External Entity Description. Again, this is only one example, the format being dependent upon the tools available to the project.

Id	Name	Description
d	Driver	EU-Rent employee based at a service depot. Assigned to move cars between his/her service depot and branches, for maintenance, and from branches served by his depot to other branches, for transfer.

Figure 2-19 External Entity Description.

2.2.4 Input/Output Descriptions

Input/Output Descriptions (I/O Descriptions) describe data flows crossing the system boundary, listing the data items contained in the data flow. Detail of the structure of the data – such as repeating groups and optionality – need not be included, since this will be rigorously defined later during Function Definition (see Chapter 3). However, it is useful to make note of such detail, as comments, during analysis. Only bottom-level input and output data flows need be documented.

Figure 2-20 gives an example of an I/O Description. Again, this is only one example, the format being dependent upon the tools available to the project.

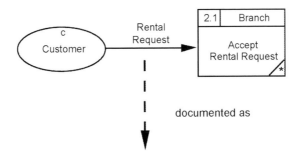

From	To	Data Flow Name	Data Content	Comment
c	2.1	Rental Request	Car Group	
			Branch [pick up from]	
			Rental Start Date	
			Rental End Date	
			Branch [return to]	only for one-way rental
			Customer Name	
			Customer Address	
			Customer Telephone	

Figure 2-20 I/O Description

2.2.5 Cross-referencing Products

Logical Data Store/Entity Cross-reference,

The Logical Data Store/Entity Cross-reference maps the correspondence between data stores in the Data Flow Diagrams and entities in the Logical Data Model[1]. This is only used to support the Logical and Required System Data Flow Diagrams, not the Current Physical Data Flow Diagrams.

Each main data store in the Logical and Required System Data Flow Models must be related to a whole number of entities on the Logical Data Model (one or more). Each entity from the Logical Data Model must belong to only one data store.

---

[1] For more details about the Logical Data Model, see the *Data Modelling* volume in this series.

Figure 2-21 gives an example of part of a Logical Data Store/Entity Cross-reference. It should be stressed that this is only one example, the format being dependent upon the tools available to the project.

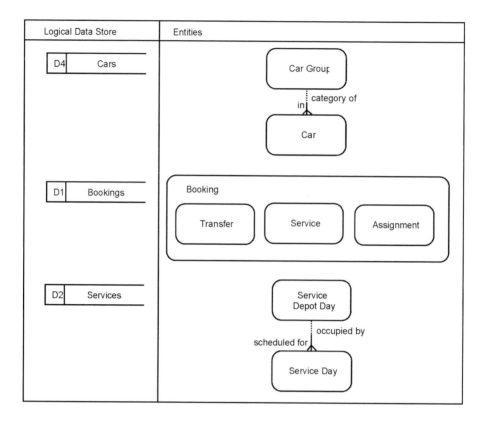

Figure 2-21 Logical Data Store/Entity Cross-reference

2.2.6 Products using Data Flow Modelling Notation

Overview Data Flow Diagram

During project initiation, it may be useful to develop a 'first cut' Level 1 Data Flow Diagram as an aid to identifying the scope and boundary of the investigation and to give an indication of the complexity of the project as an input to estimating and planning. This may be subsequently used as a basis for the Current Physical Data Flow Model.

Context Diagram

A Context Diagram, as shown in Figure 2-22, may be drawn if the initial scope of the system is not clear. The diagram concentrates on the major inputs and outputs of the system and shows clearly the external sources and recipients of data which become external entities in the Data Flow Diagrams. By concentrating on these, the scope and boundaries of the system to be investigated can be discussed and agreed with users.

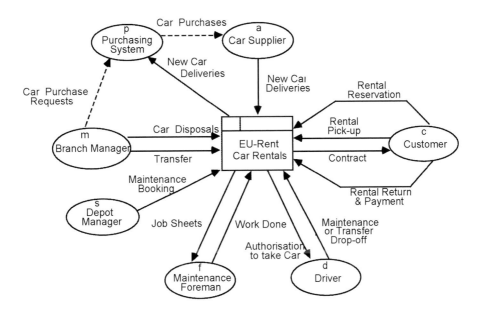

Figure 2-22 Context Diagram

BSO Data Flow Diagrams

When deciding on the scope of system development during Business System Options (see the *SSADM Foundation* volume in this series), a set of Level 1 Data Flow Diagrams may be constructed to demonstrate the differences between the options. This is discussed further in the *SSADM Foundation* volume.

2.3   The Data Flow Modelling Technique

The Data Flow Modelling technique consists of producing the three variants of the Data Flow Model described above:

- Current Physical Data Flow Model;
- Logical Data Flow Model;
- Required System Data Flow Model.

Each of these is described, in turn, below.

2.3.1 Developing the Current Physical Data Flow Model

The Current Physical Data Flow Model is developed early in the project as one of the first activities of the investigation. The use of a diagrammatic model gives a precise and concise representation of the current system that can be used as the basis of discussions between analysts and users and as an input to identifying the requirements for the new system. Effective communication between analyst and user is vital and will help to ensure that users are fully involved in the project.

The main objective of building this model is to:

- help the analysts understand the current system and the business it supports;

- accurately reflect the current environment in terms of information flow, so that all problems with current services can be identified and agreed on, then expressed as requirements in the Requirements Catalogue.

Existing services that must be supported in the new system are also identified and described.

This activity will help communication between analyst and user and will help users to be involved in the project.

Getting Started

Developing a Current Physical Data Flow Model from scratch can be very difficult when faced by a very complex system. There are various ways of approaching the task, depending upon the type of system:

- the Data Flow Model can be developed directly by interviewing key users in different areas and building a set of Data Flow Diagrams incrementally. An input to this activity which has been found useful on projects is the organisation chart which often identifies the different functional areas within an organisation;

- a Context Diagram can be used to initially identify the system boundary and the main sources and recipients of information outside the system boundary. This can then be elaborated into the Level 1 Data Flow Diagram.

- Document Flow Diagrams are a useful starting point when the system contains a significant number of different documents which are used to transmit information to different participants inside and outside the system;

- Resource Flow Diagrams are a useful starting point when the system is required to track the movement of physical goods or items around the system.

The last three of these are explained in detail below.

Developing Document Flow Diagrams

The activities in the construction of a Document Flow Diagram are:

- list major documents and information flows for the system;

- draw document flows;

- agree system boundary;

- identify processes within the system.

List major documents and information flows

All the major flows of information should be identified. This includes information flows to and from external bodies and flows internal to the system. Within the EU-Rent system, some of the main documents and information flows are as follows:

- Rental Reservation Form;

- Maintenance Booking Form;

- Transfer Booking Form;

- Driver Authorisation;

- Job Sheets;

- Contract;

- Car Documents;

- New Car Delivery Notes;

- Maintenance Drop-off note;

- Car Disposals.

Draw document flows

For each document or information flow, decide the source and the recipient. These could be parts of the organisation, people outside the organisation, other computer systems or organisations.

The documents listed above are transmitted between the following sources and recipients:

- Customer;

- Depot Manager;

- Branch staff;

- Branch Manager;

- Car Supplier;

- Service Depot;

- Purchasing System;

- Driver.

The source and recipient names are placed in ovals (similar to external entities) on a page and each of the main documents listed above are matched to the relevant sources and recipients. For example, a Rental Reservation Form is sent from a Customer to the Brach staff and the Car Documents are then given to the Customer by the Branch staff. The resulting Document Flow Diagram is shown in Figure 2-23.

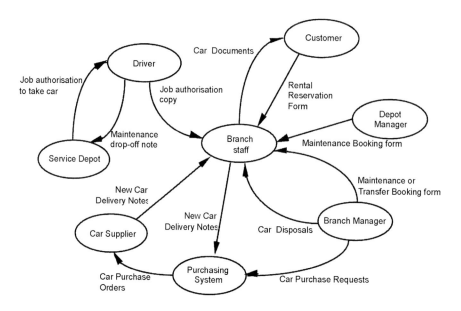

Figure 2-23 Document Flow Diagram

Other major documents that have been missed may be revealed by discussing the Document Flow Diagram with users.

Agree system boundary

The Document Flow Diagram can be shown to the users at this point for comments on its accuracy and to ensure that no area of importance is missing. The boundaries of the investigation can then be denoted on the Document Flow Diagram showing which areas are to be included in the investigation and which are to be considered as external to the system. This is represented in Figure 2-24.

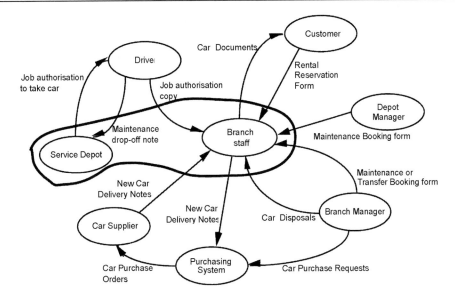

Figure 2-24 Document Flow Diagram with Investigation Boundary marked

This boundary shows the areas that may require some form of automated support. It does not necessarily indicate the boundary of a new computer system.

It may also be possible that only certain business functions performed by an area of the organisation will be automated. Even so, the area should be included inside the boundary and the scope of the automated system will be decided later.

Identify processes within the system

The activities related to the sending, receiving and processing of the major documents are represented as processes on the Current Physical Data Flow Diagrams. Where the documents are held in files or other repositories, data stores are added to the diagram. All sources or recipients outside the boundary will remain as external entities. All sources, recipients and flows inside the boundary will be transformed into processes and data flows.

A small area of the Document Flow Diagram above has been used in Figure 2-25 to demonstrate this.

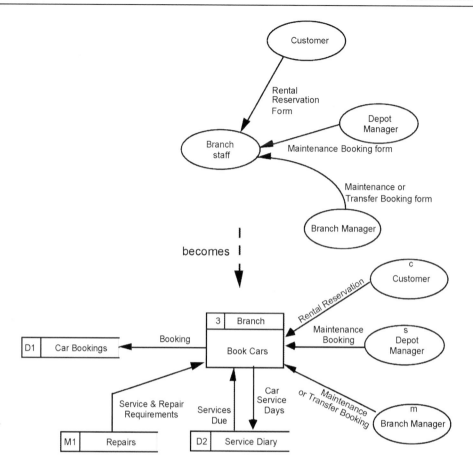

Figure 2-25 Conversion of Document Flow Diagram into Current Physical Data Flow Diagram

Hints and Tips

A Document Flow Diagram can be built up either as a single diagram or as a combination of several partial views. The combination of several partial views is a useful approach if the investigation spans several different areas of an organisation or the investigation is undertaken by more than one analyst.

An alternative approach is to follow the progress of individual documents between all their sources and recipients, drawing partial views and merging them. This is most useful for current environments that are complex and in which documents go to a number of destinations. Charting the progress of individual documents is a useful investigative technique. Individual document flows can be produced for complex or critical documents and for checking or expanding a complex Data Flow Diagram.

Developing Resource Flow Diagrams

A Resource Flow Diagram follows the movement of physical resources around a system
for which an information support system is required. The physical resources could be stock
items in a warehouse, vehicles moving in and out of a physical holding area or files being
stored in filing cabinets. It is useful to model resource flows and stores only if the physical
location of the resources is going to be of interest to the system. The technique is most
often used where the new system is required to track the location of the resources and store
information about them.

Constructing a Resource Flow Diagram

In the EU-Rent system, although the main business of the system is about car rentals, it
will also be of interest to know where each car is located physically at any one time during
servicing and maintenance in the depot in order to plan their movements. To model this,
the movement of the car from the driver (who is considered external to the system) to the
depot, into the garage awaiting maintenance, through to its final exit back to the driver can
be tracked using resource flows and resource stores. As a result, a resource flow diagram
covering movements within the depot area of the EU-Rent system could be constructed as
shown in Figure 2-26.

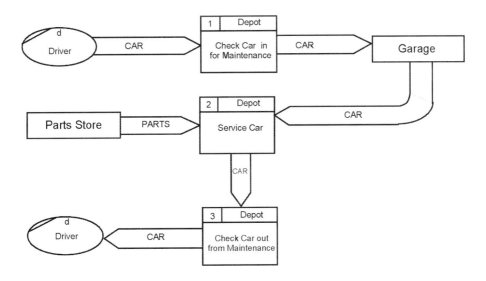

Figure 2-26 Resource Flow Diagram for maintenance area of EU-Rent

Conversion to a Data Flow Diagram

An information flow may follow the route of a resource flow, for example, the information
contained in the accompanying docket. Such information flows should be noted on the
diagram as shown in Figure 2-27.

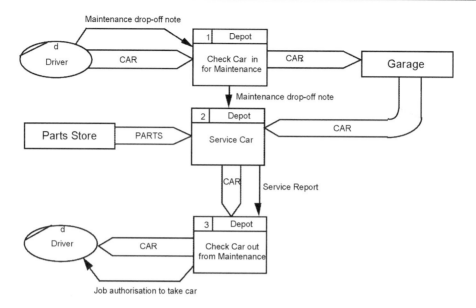

Figure 2-27 Physical Resource Flow Diagram with Data Flows

The new system is likely to be more concerned with the information flow than the resource flow, so the resource flows can be removed from the Data Flow Diagram where there are equivalent information flows.

Hints and Tips

In some environments, the actual presence of goods may be the only information available. If there is no information flow, it is acceptable to leave the resource flows on the Current Physical Data Flow Diagrams, in order to place the diagram in context: they will be removed at logicalisation.

Construction and use of the Context Diagram

A Context Diagram, as shown in Figure 2-22, may be drawn if the initial scope of the system is not clear. The diagram which treats the whole system as a single process concentrates on the major inputs and outputs of the system and shows clearly the external sources and recipients of data which become external entities in the Data Flow Diagrams. By concentrating on these, the scope and boundary of the system to be investigated can be discussed and agreed with users.

A Context Diagram is constructed by simply drawing the entire system as a single process surrounded by the external entities of the system. The major inputs and outputs are represented as data flows between these symbols.

In discussion with the users, this diagram will help to focus attention on the system boundary and the interfaces to other systems or external agencies. Once this diagram is agreed, the processes for the Level 1 Data Flow Diagram can be derived. This is done by identifying groups of related input and output data flows from the Context Diagram and deducing the processes that would deal with them.

2.3.2 Developing the Logical Data Flow Model

If there is an existing system, it may have evolved over a period of time and have been constrained by:

- politics;

- out-of-date equipment;

- toleration of deficiencies;

- dispersed operational locations.

The analyst should draw a logical model of the current services, free of such constraints. The aim is to remove duplication in processing and data stores, and to re-group bottom-level processes into the functional areas that the user requires. The Logical Data Flow Model is created from the Current Physical Data Flow Model, by carrying out specific activities.

The main activities of logicalisation are:

- rationalise data stores;

- rationalise bottom-level processes;

- regroup bottom-level processes;

- check the Logical Data Flow Diagrams for consistency and completeness.

Some or all of these activities may have to be repeated, to ensure that the resulting model is fully logical and consistent.

Rationalise data stores

Data stores in the Current Physical Data Flow Diagrams represent the actual ways in which data is held. The EU-Rent system has data stores such as 'Service Diary' and 'Customer Blacklist'. These are terms familiar to the user from the current environment, but may not be logical groupings of data. Data may be duplicated between them.

Main logical data stores are derived from the Current Environment Logical Data Model (LDM). The main data stores on the Logical Data Flow Diagrams must reflect the data content of the entities of the Current Environment Logical Data Model. Each main logical data store is related to an entity or group of entities in the Logical Data Model[2].

---

[2] For more details on the Current Environment Logical Data Model, see the *Data Modelling* volume in this series.

If the entity groupings are not obvious, then look for entities which are:

- linked via relationships;

- created together;

- part of the same major inputs or outputs to the system;

- capable of description by a single term, for example, accounts.

It would be possible to create a data store for each entity in the Logical Data Model but it is better to keep the groupings of data at a more summary level on the Data Flow Diagrams, as the detailed definition of the data is held in the Logical Data Model.

Ultimately, each main data store must correspond to an entity or group of entities in the Current Environment Logical Data Model and entity in the Logical Data Model must be held completely within one and only one main data store.

The correspondence between entities and data stores is documented using the Logical Data Store/Entity Cross-reference.

The Logical Data Structure from the EU-Rent system with groupings of entities into logical data stores is shown in Figure 2-28. Here, the groupings are indicated by shading.

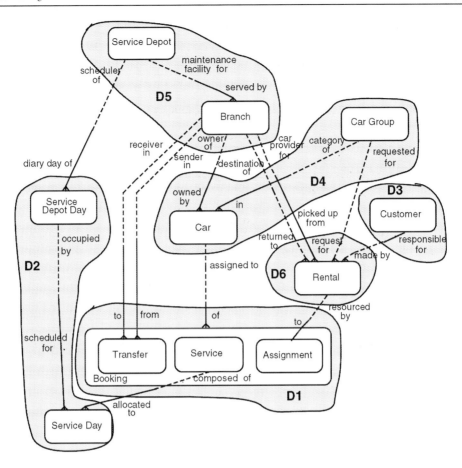

Figure 2-28 Identifying Logical Data Stores

These groupings are documented on the Logical Data Store/Entity Cross-reference as shown in Figure 2-29.

Logical Data Store	Entities
D1: Bookings	Booking
D2: Services	Service Depot Day Service Day
D3: Customers	Customer
D4: Cars	Car Group Car
D5: Locations	Service Depot Branch
D6: Rentals	Rental

Figure 2-29 Logical Data Store/Entity Cross-reference

Main Data Stores on the Current Physical Data Flow Diagrams can be cross-referenced to the Main Data Stores which have been derived from the Logical Data Model using an intermediate product: the Logical/Physical Data Store Cross-reference. This will help to check that all the data held in the current system is still represented in the Logical Data Flow Model. An example Logical/Physical Data Store Cross-reference is shown in Figure 2-30.

Physical Data Store	Logical Data Store
D1: Car Bookings (bookings)	D1: Bookings
D2: Service Diary	D2: Services
D3: Customer Blacklist	D3: Customers
D1: Car Bookings (cars and groups) M1: Repairs M1/1: Car Deliveries	D4: Cars
D1: Car Bookings (branch locations) D2: Service Diary (depot locations)	D5: Locations
D2/1: Reservations	D6: Rentals
T1: Day Reservations	T1: Day Reservations
T2/1(M): Reservation Forms	not needed
T5/1(M): Late Returns List	Replaced by ad-hoc query
M5.1/1: Claims	Replaced by system-initiated report
M3.7/1: Maintenance Manuals	Outside boundary of automatable system

Figure 2-30 Logical/Physical Data Store Cross-reference for the EU-Rent system

A transient data store should only remain in the Logical Data Flow Diagram where a process requires a complete batch of data and perhaps waits for a separate input (a manager's authorisation for example) before running.

The major difference between the two types of data store is that a main data store corresponds to entities on the Logical Data Model, a transient data store does not. The analyst must examine the transient data stores to see whether they are still logically necessary. It is possible that a transient store only exists in the current system because of some physical constraint.

Rationalise bottom-level processes

Logical Data Flow Diagrams should represent the processing that is logically taking place within the current system. It is not possible to offer an exhaustive list of rules for deriving logical processes, but these guidelines may help:

- a logical process should transform or use data because the business requires it to. This will be irrespective of how it is implemented. For example, if a process is only re-organising data it should be removed;

- a logical process should show what is being done, not where and by whom. Location should be irrelevant on a Logical Data Flow Model and therefore all references to location are removed in logicalisation;

- where a process is retrieving data only to display or print, remove it from the diagram, but check whether the retrieval is already in the Requirements Catalogue, and, if not, enter it. Retaining the retrieval in the Data Flow Model is justifiable only if it is a major element of the system's functionality and it will help in user understanding (e.g., printing out the rental certificate to be given to the customer);

- where data remains unaltered by a process then that process should be replaced by a data flow;

- where possible, processes which perform identical activities should be combined;

- where two or more processes are always performed together or as a series, they should if possible be combined. An example of this would be where data is validated initially by one office prior to being passed to another office for further validation and recording. In the Current Physical Data Flow Model there would be two processes. The Logical Data Flow Diagram should show one combined process;

- where a process exists on the Current Physical Data Flow Diagrams purely because the data is currently held in many different places this should be removed. All data is now held only once in the Logical Data Flow Model and there is no need for processes to maintain consistencies between separate copies of the same data;

- where a process describes an element of work that requires some subjective decision making, or is an activity that is legally required to be done by a person, the process should be split. The external element of the work is represented by an external entity and data flows communicating with the process;

- where a process contains functionality that also occurs in other processes, it may be necessary to represent the duplicated and common element in a common elementary processing description, referenced by all bottom-level processes that use it.

Rationalising processes may require a number of iterations before a fully logical view is reached. As processes are rationalised, logically redundant data flows between processes should also be removed.

In the EU-Rent system, the Current Physical Data Flow Model contains a process which batches up rental requests as they are received. Batches of forms are processed on a regular basis. This is represented in Figure 2-31 by a transient data store which is used to collect the forms as they arrive followed by a process which deals with the forms.

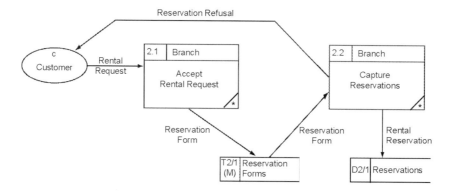

Figure 2-31 extract from Current Physical Data Flow Diagrams showing batching of rental requests

The separation of process 2.1 and 2.2 in the diagram above is only necessary because of organisational constraints. Logically, rental requests can be dealt with as they are received. This is represented in the Logical Data Flow Model as shown in Figure 2-32.

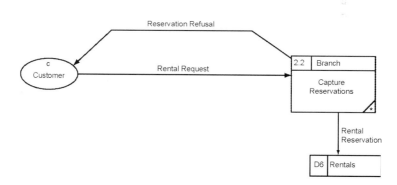

Figure 2-32 Removal of logically unnecessary process and transient data store

This is still not quite right, however, as the input is still shown as coming direct from the Customer. The boundary of the system should be between the direct users of the system (potential user roles) and processes. An external entity is inserted between the Customer external entity and the process as shown in Figure 2-33 to indicate that the Booking Clerk will be responsible for recording details about reservations and being notified of refusals. In this way, the Logical Data Flow Model starts to identify the boundary between the business system and the automated system.

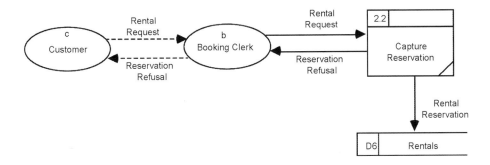

Figure 2-33 Insertion of Booking Clerk as external entity

Reconstruct the Data Flow Diagram hierarchy

After the rationalisation of the bottom-level processes, it is necessary to group these processes into higher-level processes to reintroduce the levels of Data Flow Diagram up to Level 1. This produces a completely logical set of Data Flow Diagrams on which the Required System Data Flow Diagrams will be based. The processes at the top level will no longer show the separation of functional areas based upon existing organisational constraints. Instead, they will reflect a logical view.

It is not easy to define what constitutes a 'logical' grouping. The derivation of groupings should be based on the users' perception of the different functional areas of the system. The users' perception of the way the system should be divided into functional areas might be based around the organisational structure. This should be taken into account when identifying groupings of processes.

Grouping may also be based on the following:

- identifying similarity of type between the different low-level processes. There will be two main types of process which will not normally be mixed in the same grouping:

  - those which support the business of the system;

  - those which maintain reference data and deal with housekeeping tasks.

- grouping processes that access the same data. As an aid to identifying processes that operate on the same data, it is useful to draw up the working document, the Process/Entity Matrix (see Figure 2-34). The correspondence between processes and entities can be derived using the Logical Data Store/Entity Cross-reference; the usage of data stores by processes is reflected on the Data Flow Diagrams. If a process accesses several different entities, it is necessary to decide priorities for grouping. Usually, the entities updated are more important than those that are just read. After this, if a process updates a number of entities from different data stores, it is necessary to look at the main purpose of the process to decide which update is the highest priority.

ENTITY/ PROCESS	Service Depot	Branch	Car	Customer	Rental Booking
Accept Rental Request			R	R	U
Cancel Reservation					U
Book Car			U	R	U
Arrange Maintenance	R		U		
Accept Rental Return			U		U
Check Car in for Maintenance	R		U		
Set Rental Rates		R	U		
Blacklist Customers				U	

Figure 2-34 Process/Entity Matrix

By far the most important factor is the user's view of the different functional areas. Very often current system grouping will be associated with data accessed and process types. Whichever view is used as a starting point, the result must support the 'logical' functional areas which meet the user's business needs.

After the grouping exercise, it is possible that there are some process-to-process data flows at the top level due to some processing being common to several different areas. If this happens, it is preferable to remove the process altogether and describe it as a common Elementary Process Description, referencing it in the Elementary Process Description of each bottom-level process that performs that functionality.

Check the Logical Data Flow Diagrams for consistency and completeness

Once the tasks of logicalisation have been completed it is important to ensure that all the data flows, processes and data stores in the Current Physical Data Flow Diagrams are accounted for. Where components have been removed, the reason for their deletion should be documented.

The Level 1 Current Physical Data Flow Diagram is shown in Figure 2-35.

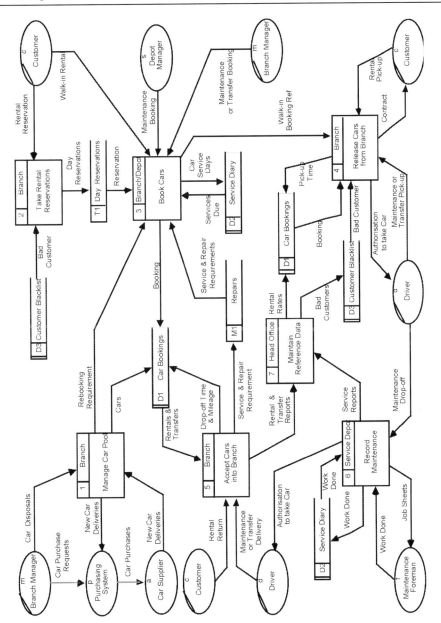

Figure 2-35 Level 1 Current Physical Data Flow Diagram

The resulting Level 1 Logical Data Flow Diagram is shown in Figure 2-36.

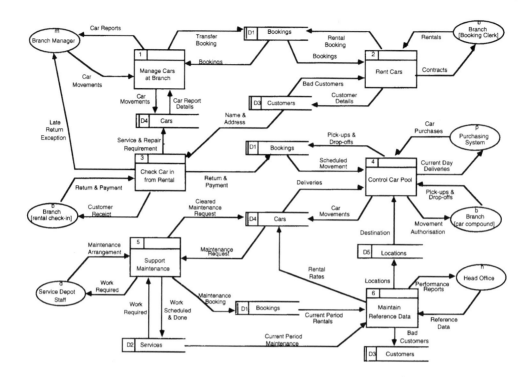

Figure 2-36 Level 1 Logical Data Flow Diagram

2.3.3 Developing the Required System Data Flow Model

The Required System Data Flow Model is based on one of the following:

- the Logical Data Flow Model, tailored to meet the scope of the Selected Business System Option and to satisfy the requirements recorded in the Requirements Catalogue;

- the Data Flow Diagram which supports the selected Business System Option (see the *SSADM Foundation* volume in this series);

- the Business Activity Model which identifies the essential activities that must be performed in support of the new system.

There are no specific guidelines for developing the Required System Data Flow Model but the following should be borne in mind during its development:

- the Data Flow Model will be used to assist in the identification of functions and events so should be structured to assist in this activity;

- the flows to and from external entities will provide the data items that will form the basis for the user interface;

- the external entities may be used as an input to identifying user roles.

The analyst should ensure that the Required System Data Flow Model will support Function Definition (see Chapter 3) by checking that:

- there is one driving input to a process;

- there are a minimum of inter-process data flows;

- there is no attempt to model error-correction dialogues, since this is the concern of Function Definition (at a high level) and (at a more detailed level) later techniques – Conceptual Process Modelling for integrity errors and physical process specification for syntactic errors.

The complete Required System Data Flow Model is shown below in Figure 2-37

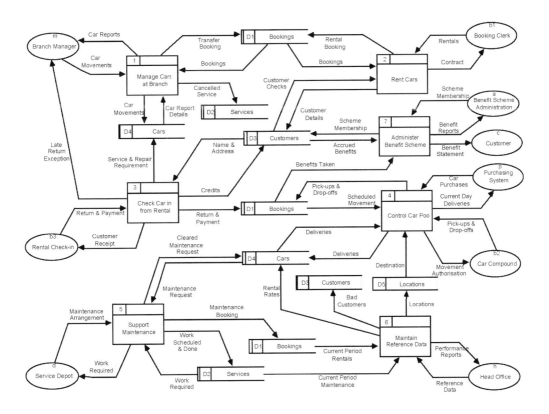

Figure 2-37 Level 1 Required System Data Flow Model

2.4   Relationships with other techniques

2.4.1 Logical Data Modelling (covered in the Data Modelling volume)

The Data Flow Model is developed in parallel with the Logical Data Model, so the two models must be kept consistent with each other.

The Current Physical Data Flow Model is developed in parallel with the Current Environment Logical Data Model (LDM) and the Required System Logical Data Model in parallel with the Required Logical Data Model. The analyst must ensure that data in the Logical Data Model entities is represented in data stores and input data flows in the Data Flow Model. This correspondence is done formally when logical data stores are identified by grouping the entities of the Logical Data Structure and the correspondence documented in the Logical Data Store/Entity Cross-reference.

2.4.2 Business Activity Modelling (covered in The Business Context volume)

Business Activity Modelling influences the role of the Current Physical Data Flow Model as they are both modelling the same business system in slightly different ways:

- the Current Physical Data Flow Model provides one route for discovering the business activities – "this is what we do now - what business activities are we supporting?";

- Business Activity Modelling provides a more systematic approach to investigating the possibilities of reuse of parts of existing systems. It investigates the business requirements and can be used to evaluate the Current Physical Data Flow Model, asking the question "is what we are doing now adequate to support the business need?". Even where existing code cannot be re-used, specifications may be re-usable.

The use of Current Physical Data Flow Models allows the analyst to understand the detail of what is currently happening in the area under investigation and provides a means of checking with the user what data is being used and what processes are being performed. However, it often causes problems when the analyst is required to take an objective view of the underlying data and processes during logicalisation as this requires a complete switch in thinking. The development of a Business Activity Model approaches the system from an entirely different viewpoint and allows the analyst to model the essential activities of the system without becoming too involved in the detail of what is actually going on. These two different views are both very useful and can be used to complement one another in the investigation of the system.

The use of a Business Activity Model may modify the way in which the Current Physical and Logical Data Flow Models are used within a project. There may be no requirement to transform the Logical Data Flow Model into the Required System Data Flow Model. Instead, the Required System Data Flow Model can be based upon the Work Practice Model, which is the mapping of the Business Activity Model onto the user organisation.

2.4.3 Requirements Definition (covered in **The Business Context** *volume*)

The Requirements Catalogue is updated with references to the objects on the Data Flow Model which support the required functionality.

The analyst must ensure that the requirements given in the Requirements Catalogue and confirmed in Business System Options can be supported by the inputs, outputs, data entities and functionality represented in the model.

2.4.4 Business System Options (covered in the **SSADM Foundation** *volume*)

The Logical Data Flow Model is used as an input to the derivation of the different Business System Options. Each option would normally be documented using (at least) a top level Data Flow Diagram which can be used to show the boundary of the proposed system.

2.4.5 Work Practice Modelling (covered in the **User Centred Design** *volume*)

The Current Physical Data Flow Model can be used as a source of information about the current tasks. This is then used as an input to Task Modelling.

2.4.6 Function Definition (covered in **Chapter 3**)

The objective of constructing the Required Data Flow Model is to facilitate Function Definition. The Required System Data Flow Model can be modified where required if new events and functions are not supported by the inputs, processes and updates of data already shown.

2.4.7 Entity Behaviour Modelling (covered in the **Behaviour and Process Modelling** *volume*)

A data flow generally contains one event or a batch of events. Analysts who set out to validate the Required System Data Flow Model with this in mind will naturally be concerned about the correspondence between input data flows and events. Events may be identified from the Required System Data Flow Model with reference to updates to main data stores. Further events, and possibly more functions, are identified when Entity Life Histories are created. This may lead to updating of the Required System Data Flow Model if this is considered to be helpful.

2.4.8 User Role Definition (covered in the User Centred Design *volume)*

There are two types of external entity on the Required System Data Flow Diagrams: those that are external to the entire system and those that are part of the system but external to the automated part. The second type equate to system users. As the Required System Data Flow Model is developed, the external entities that equate to system users should be tied to user roles.

3   FUNCTION DEFINITION

Function Definition identifies units of processing specification, or functions, which need to be controlled as a whole in order to support the users' tasks.

During the development project two types of function are identified;

- **On-line functions**, where the user interfaces directly with the system either to update some of the information stored within the system or to retrieve information stored by the system or, more normally, a combination of the two.

- **Off-line functions**, where the system operates without user intervention (e.g., back-up). This type of function is sometimes known as a Batch function.

This manual deals solely with off-line functions. On-line functions are described in the *User Centred Design* volume which is part of this series.

3.1   Concepts of Function Definition

Function Definition has several purposes:

- it identifies and defines the units of processing specification required to support user tasks which need to be carried forward to physical design;

- it pulls together the products of analysis and design, which together specify a function;

- it develops and confirms a common understanding between the analyst and the user of how the system processing is to be organised;

- it provides a basis for sizing and for deriving design objectives.

A function is a unit of off-line processing which is required to be controlled as a unit in support of a single task. Where the task requires several units of off-line processing which do not directly interact, and do not need to be controlled together, there will be more than one function defined for that task.

Functions can contain elements which are either on-line or off-line (batch). The function elements which are on-line require a user interface and are therefore defined in a different way from function elements which operate without a user interface (see the Function Definition chapter in the *User Centred Design* volume in this series).

Off-line functions can be identified in one of a number of ways:

- by looking at the Required System Data Flow Model;

- from the Requirements Catalogue;

- from the Required Task Models (see the *User Centred Design* volume in this series) where they are initiated from within human activities;

- by consideration of input/output streams which will need to be accepted/generated as a batch.

The interrelationships between functions and other analysis and design products and components are shown in Figure 3-1.

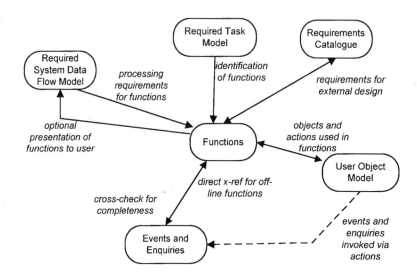

Figure 3-1 Relationship between functions and other analysis and design products

3.2   Products of Function Definition

The main product of the Function Definition technique is the Function Description.

All functions are documented by a largely textual document called the Function Description. This describes the important features of the function and details cross-references to related products. If thought useful this can be supplemented by a I/O Structure which documents the input and output data streams for the function.

3.2.1 Function Description

A Function Description contains some descriptive text and a large number of cross-references to other products. The precise format of the product will depend upon the needs of the project and the tools available for documenting functions. An example of a typical Function Description for an off-line function is given in Figure 3-2.

Function ID and Name: F54 – Produce Car Stock Report	
Function Type	Implementation Type: Off-line Process Type: Enquiry Initiation Type: User initiated
Task x-ref	395: Manage stock levels
Common Function Component x-ref	None
Function Text	A report is produced on an ad hoc basis for the Branch Manager and Purchasing department detailing all cars held in stock at a given branch.
Potential Problems	None
DFD Process x-ref	N/A
I/O Description x-ref	N/A
Requirements Catalogue entries x-ref	0045: Provide information on car stocks in branches to support car pool management
I/O Structure x-ref	Branch Stocks
Related functions	022: Report Deliveries is a regular daily report which contains similar information presented in a similar format.
Events and enquiries x-ref	Enquiry: Branch Stocks enquiry
Event/enquiry frequency	1 per function
Volumes	Ad hoc, expected no more than once per week
Service Level Requirements	Must be available in office hours at any time. Report should complete printing in less than 15 minutes.

Figure 3-2 Example of Function Description

The properties of a function that are recorded on a Function Description for an off-line function are as follows:

- **Function ID**. A unique identifier;

- **Function name**. A name that describes the processing contained in the function;

- **Function Type**. There are three ways of classifying functions. Each function should have an entry for all three classifications;

  - **Implementation Type** – in this case it is always 'off-line';

  - **Process Type** – either update or enquiry (U or E);

- ■ **Initiation Type** – either user or system (U or S) – where the initiation type is 'system' the function would usually be 'off-line'.

- **Cross-reference to task or sub-task**. If the function is one-to-one with a task, this is a reference to that task. If the function covers only one sub-task within a task, or a common sub-task, this reference is put here;

- **Function Text**. A brief description of the function including what causes the function to be invoked, what the system does in response to that input and the output produced by the function;

- **Potential problems**. An overview of any exceptions that may be encountered during the execution of the function. This should be used as an informal way of noting down information as it is discovered;

- **Cross-reference to DFD processes**. The bottom-level DFD processes covered by the function;

- **Cross-reference to I/O Descriptions**. The I/O Descriptions covered by the function;

- **Cross-reference to Requirements Catalogue**. The Requirements Catalogue entries satisfied by this function;

- **Cross-reference to I/O Structures**. This is used for off-line elements of functions only and is used to pull together all I/O Structures for the same function;

- **Related functions**. A reference to any related function. An example is where an off-line function stores errors on a transient data store. The errors are later corrected on-line. Two functions would be created but cross-referenced to each other;

- **Cross-reference to events and enquiries**. The events and enquiries handled by the function;

- **Event/enquiry frequency**. For each event/enquiry within the function the frequency of the event/ enquiry in relation to the function. This will usually be 1. However, if there is more than one event/ enquiry in a function and some of those events/ enquiries are mutually exclusive or optional, then the frequency of those events/ enquiries will be less than 1. For example, an event/enquiry which is invoked on only half the occasions when the function is invoked will have a frequency of 0.5. The frequency of an event/enquiry that is iterated within a function will be greater than 1;

- **Volumes** (frequency of use of function). A clear indication should be given of the number of occurrences of the function being used in a given time period – this will be based on the frequency of tasks. If there are any significant peaks or troughs anticipated, in any time cycle, these should be noted. For example, the same function could undergo seasonal fluctuations through the year, more local fluctuations on a monthly basis and have peaks and troughs through the working day. This volumetric information will be needed to assess the viability of the Service Level Requirements and to predict the capacity requirements during Technical System Options;

- **Service Level Requirements**. These should bear a close similarity to the non-functional requirements from the Requirements Catalogue entries the function satisfies and consist of the following:

  - **Description** (textual description of the service level requirement);

  - **Target Value** (quantitative expression of performance, size, cost satisfaction levels, etc.).

3.2.2 I/O Structures

Input/Output (I/O) Structures, consist of an I/O Structure Diagram and an optional I/O Structure Element Description:

- **I/O Structure Diagrams** are a pictorial representation of the data items which are input to a function or output from a function;

- **I/O Structure Element Descriptions** are the backing documentation for an I/O Structure Diagram and list the data items represented by each element of the I/O Structure Diagram.

I/O Structure Diagrams use Jackson-like notation with sequences, selections and iterations represented. Figure 3-3 illustrates the structure conventions for I/O Structure Diagrams.

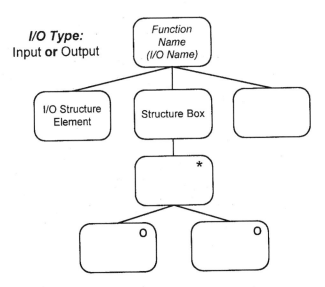

Figure 3-3 Conventions for I/O Structure Diagrams

All boxes on the diagram are 'soft' boxes. The top box of the structure contains the function name for which the I/O Structure Diagram has been developed and the name of the input or output if more than one I/O Structure is developed for the function.

A structure is built up using the following components:

- sequence represented by a box with a series of plain boxes below it: the plain boxes should be read from left to right;

- iteration represented by a box with a single box containing an asterisk in the top right corner: this box can be repeated a number of times from zero to many;

- selection represented by series of boxes, each of which contains 'o' in the top right corner: these boxes are alternatives for one another, only one of which will be selected at this point in the structure.

Each I/O Structure element (bottom leaf of the structure) represents one or more data items which cross the system boundary, and is given a descriptive name (if two or more I/O Structure elements contain the same set of data items, they should be given the same name). The following rules apply to the identification of I/O Structure elements:

- repeating groups of data items are not combined with items outside the group;

- mandatory and optional items are not grouped together.

An example of an I/O Structure from the EU-Rent system is shown in Figure 3-4.

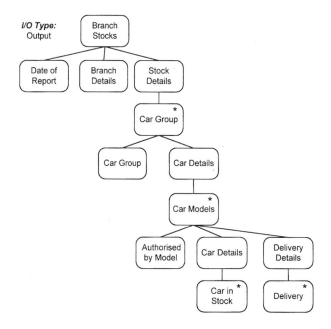

Figure 3-4 Example I/O Structure from the EU-Rent system: Branch Stocks

The I/O Structure Diagram can be supplemented using the I/O Structure Element Description. An I/O Structure Element Description is a central list of all I/O Structure elements which appear on all I/O Structures together with the set of data items represented by the box. Comments may be added to the general description of the I/O Structure element or to its appearance in a particular I/O Structure.

An example extract from an I/O Element Description developed to support the I/O Structure shown in Figure 3-4 is shown in Figure 3-5.

I/O Structure Element Name	Data Items	Comments
Report Date	Date report printed	system generated
Branch Details	Branch ID Branch Name	
Car Group	Group Code	
Authorised by Model	Model ID Model Name Manufacturer Name Number Authorised	
Car in Stock	Registration Number Colour Purchase Date	
Delivery	Purchase Ref Delivery Quantity Delivery Date	

Figure 3-5 Example I/O Structure Element Description

3.3   The Function Definition Technique

Function Definition consists of a number of activities which are as follows:

- identify functions;

- specify functions;

- produce I/O Structures.

These activities are described in more detail in the following paragraphs.

3.3.1 Identify functions

Off-line functions can be identified in one of a number of ways:

- from the Required System Data Flow Model;

- from the Requirements Catalogue (for Enquiry Functions);

- from events and enquiries;

- by consideration of input/output streams which will need to be accepted/generated as a batch;

- from discussion with users.

Functions from the Required System Data Flow Model

Functions can be identified from the Required System Data Flow Model by looking at the bottom-level Data Flow Diagrams and finding processes which do not receive data from an external entity representing a user role. This can include processes which receive input from external entities representing other systems, processes with inputs only from data stores and processes which output data to all types of external entity. When this type of process has been found, the function will be identified by tracing through from driving inputs to corresponding outputs and including any accesses to data stores. The aim is to identify all the processes, output data flows and updates to data stores that are performed in response to an input data flow before all the data on the input data flow has been processed.

An example from the EU-Rent system is the function which allocates cars to advance bookings. This function is performed each night when the advance bookings for the next day are processed in a batch. The Data Flow Diagram showing this process is shown in Figure 3-6.

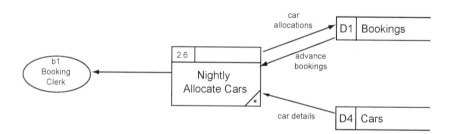

Figure 3-6 Function identified from Data Flow Diagram

It should be noted that although the example above shows one function being derived from one process this is not necessary and one function can cover a number of processes and vice versa.

Functions from the Requirements Catalogue

The Requirements Catalogue will contain information about the functionality required from the new automated system. The update functionality should be represented in the Required System Data Flow Model. An evaluation of the Requirements Catalogue will help to ensure that all the update functions required have been identified.

The main set of functions that will be identified directly from the Requirements Catalogue are off-line enquiry functions which are not represented on the Required System Data Flow Diagrams or not explicit within the Required Task Models.

Functions from events and enquiries

Some events and enquiries may have been identified as being required and documented on the Entity Access Matrix (see the *Behaviour and Process Modelling* volume in this series). Some of these events will require off-line processing and may indicate the need for functions.

Entity Behaviour Modelling (see the *Behaviour and Process Modelling* volume in this series) may identify new events and enquiries and these will need to be checked against existing functions to ensure that each event and enquiry is covered by at least one function.

Functions from input/output data streams

The Required Task Models, Required System Data Flow Model and Requirements Catalogue should provide all the functions required. However, it is worth an overall check of all input and output data streams to ensure that they are all covered by functions (either off-line or on-line). Examples could include the generation of a tape of pay-related information to be sent to BACS or the receipt of batches of reference data such as details of changes in prices and terms to be loaded into the database.

Functions from discussions with users

In general it is advisable to involve users in the identification of functions as they will help to validate the assumptions made by analysts and ensure the functions are designed to support the users' tasks, not just the analysts' perceptions of those tasks.

3.3.2 Specify functions

As each function is identified it is documented using the Function Description.

The elementary process descriptions from the Required System Data Flow Diagrams can be used to supply detail about the underlying processing requirements of the function. The majority of functions described in the Required System Data Flow Model will be update functions but major enquiry functions may also be shown on the Required System Data Flow Diagrams.

3.3.3 Produce I/O Structures

As part of producing the Required System Data Flow Diagrams each cross-boundary input and output data flow is documented on an I/O Description. This will be a simple list of the data items carried by the flow together with any extra information that is of relevance (e.g., optionality of items, repeating groups of data items and conditionality of items).

For functions that have not been derived from the Required System Data Flow Model, it will be necessary to identify the data items that will be input to and output from the function before I/O Structures can be developed.

For each off-line function a separate I/O Structure can be produced for each individual input or output. These will probably be merged in Physical Design, but at this point the modelling of each individual I/O separately will aid the analyst.

From a definition of the data items flowing into and out of the function, a set of I/O Structures can be developed. Below are the rules to be followed in grouping data items:

- repeating groups of data items are not grouped with items outside the group;

- mandatory and optional items are not grouped together.

Using these rules, identify:

- groups of data items input to the processing;

- groups of data items that make up the system responses.

Draw the I/O Structures for each function and, if thought useful, document I/O Structure Diagrams using the I/O Structure Element Descriptions.

3.4   Relationship with other techniques

3.4.1 *Logical Data Modelling (covered in the* Data Modelling *volume)*

Enquiry functions or enquiry fragments of functions will validate that the Required System Logical Data Model can support the enquiry

3.4.2 *Entity Behaviour Modelling (covered in the* Behaviour and Process Modelling *volume)*

The identification of functions often identifies the need for events and enquiries. Conversely, the examination of events and enquiries may help to determine what functions are required.

As Event Identification and Entity Life History Analysis are carried out events will be identified. These events must be cross-referenced by functions. New functions may be created or existing functions amended.

3.4.3 User Requirements Definition (covered in The Business Context volume)

Requirements for enquiries are likely to be documented in the Requirements Catalogue. These enquiry requirements are developed into enquiries which are used by functions or components of functions.

Service level requirements may be recorded against functional requirements in the Requirements Catalogue. These are transferred to the Function Description where appropriate during Function Definition.

3.4.4 Technical System Options (covered in the SSADM Foundation volume)

Function frequency is recorded in the Function Description. This information is useful in the estimation of system sizing and can be input to the formulation of Technical System Options.

3.4.5 Physical Design (covered in the Database and Physical Process Design volume)

Functions are the units of processing specification that are input to Physical Design. The Function Definition provides, either directly or by referencing other products, a complete logical process specification for each function.

4   META-MODEL FOR FUNCTION MODELLING

The purpose of the meta-model is to explain the concepts of Business Activity Modelling and Requirements Definition. This model attempts to identify the key concepts of these areas and shows the interrelationships between the concepts. Following the diagram, there are descriptions for each of the boxes.

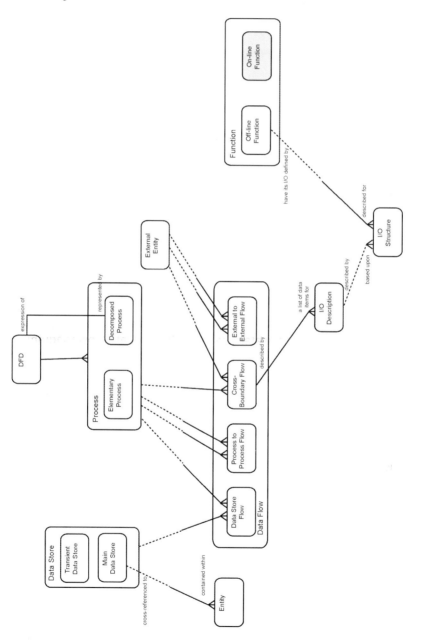

Figure 4-1 Meta-model for concepts in Function Modelling

Entity	Description
Cross-boundary Flow	A type of data flow which is sourced from or received by an external entity with a process at the other end of the flow.
Data Store Flow	A type of data flow which is sourced from or received by a data store with a process at the other end of the flow.
Decomposed Process	A process which is further decomposed within the Data Flow Diagram hierarchy. Each decomposed process will be represented by a Data Flow Diagram at the lower level.
DFD	A diagram representing the flow of information around a system, the way in which it is changed and stored and the sources and recipients of data outside the boundary of the system. Each Data Flow Diagram contains processes, data stores, external entities and data flows.
Elementary Process	A type of process that is not decomposed any further within the Data Flow Model. This type of process would normally be associated with an Elementary Process description.
Entity	Something, whether concrete or abstract, which is of relevance to the system and about which information needs to be stored.
External Entity	Whatever or whoever donates data to or receives data from the system, represented on Data Flow Diagrams as an oval.
External to External Flow	A type of data flow which represents the transmission of data between External Entities. This type of flow is considered to be outside the immediate boundary of investigation and is denoted by a dotted line.
I/O Description	A list of data items on a cross-boundary data flow.
I/O Structure	A structured representation of the data items associated with an off-line function.
Main Data Store	A data store which represents data that will be stored and altered by the system. This equates to a table within a data base.
Off-line Function	A function which involves no interaction with the user. This type of function (sometimes called a Batch Function) is System Initiated.
On-line Function	A function which involves some user interaction. This type of function is not covered within this manual. (See the *User Centred Design* volume in this series for a full description of off-line functions).

Entity	Description
Process to Process Flow	A data flow which communicates data from one process to another process.
Transient Data Store	A type of data store which is temporary, accumulating data for use by another process. The read of the data will delete it from the data store.

5   PRODUCT DESCRIPTIONS FOR FUNCTION MODELLING

Listed below are the Product Descriptions for those products produced during Data Flow
Modelling and Function Definition. These Product Descriptions should not be regarded as
definitive, rather they are a start point that can be tailored for each individual project. It is
expected that each project will examine the composition list and add and remove as
necessary to suit their particular project. In addition if a Case Tool is utilised then the Case
Tool may have a suggested list of its own.

5.1   Context Diagram

Purpose

To provide an overall view of the external data flows to/from the system. It is drawn by the analyst using Data Flow Modelling notation to represent the context in which the system operates.

Composition

The system (a single process), multiple external entities.

Links (data flows) between external entities and processes.

Position in System Development Template

Investigation.

Quality Criteria:

1   Is the diagram semantically correct?

2   Is the scope of the system clearly shown?

3   Are all known external entities represented?

4   Is there one and only one 'process' box representing the system?

External Dependencies

Users closely involved with validation.

5.2 Data Flow Diagram – Level I

Purpose

To contain the overall information flow model of the system. This will be revised during the lifetime of the system to reflect current, logical or required services.

The Level 1 Data Flow Diagram of the current system is drawn by the analyst to describe the scope of the system under investigation.

Level 1 of the Logical Data Flow Diagram is built from the bottom up, by grouping bottom-level processes into more abstract units and drawing the data flows that represent information flowing at the lower level.

Level 1 of the Required System Data Flow Diagram is reached when processes map onto a user's view of the functions that the system is intended to support.

Composition

Variant identifier – one of:

- Current Physical;

- Logical;

- Required System.

Diagram elements representing:

- Processes;

- Data flows;

- Data stores;

- External entities.

Position in System Development Template

Investigation.

Specification - External Design.

Quality Criteria:

For all:

1   Is the variant identifier properly completed?

2   Are notational conventions correctly applied?

3   Is the boundary of the system clear?

4   Are all user-perceived functional areas represented?

5   Are meaningful names used for processes and data stores?

6   Are all identifiers unique?

7   Do external entity names accurately reflect the environment outside the system?

8   Does the diagram accurately reflect the physical, logical or required system in terms of external entities, data stores and data flows?

9   Does the diagram avoid giving an inappropriate level of detail, such as sequencing or detailed processing logic?

For Logical Data Flow Diagram:

10   Are all physical aspects of the current system removed, unless they are constraints on the requirement?

11   Are any enquiries remaining after logicalisation major ones?

For Required System Data Flow Diagram:

12   Are all the facilities defined by the Selected Business System Option, and nothing else, modelled in the Required System Data Flow Diagrams?

External Dependencies

Users closely involved with validation.

5.3   Data Flow Diagrams – Lower Level

Purpose

To describe processes shown on a higher level Data Flow Diagram in more detail. The higher level may be the Level 1 Data Flow Diagram, or may be itself a Lower Level Data Flow Diagram. The process box on the lower level diagram is drawn much larger to accommodate the further processes and data stores subsumed within the higher-level process.

The external entities, data stores and other processes with which the decomposed process communicates are re-represented in this diagram outside the process boundary and the data flows that represent this communication are drawn going to the boundary of the process and, when the diagram is complete, crossing it. External entities and data stores outside the process boundary may be decomposed from higher-level objects.

Composition

A set of Data Flow Diagrams – Lower Level, each consisting of:

- Variant identifier, one of:
    - Current Physical;
    - Logical;
    - Required System.
- Details from higher level:
    - Higher level process number;
    - Higher level process name;
    - External entities;
    - Data stores from higher level;
    - Processes from higher level.
- Additional details for this level (appearing within the outer process box):
    - Data stores;
    - Processes.

Position in System Development Template

Investigation.

Specification - External Design.

Quality Criteria:

For each:

1   Is the variant correctly identified?

2   Are notational conventions correctly applied?

3   Is the boundary of the process clear?

4   Are meaningful names used for processes and data stores?

5   Do external entity names accurately reflect the environment outside the system?

6   Does the diagram avoid giving an inappropriate level of detail, such as sequencing
         or detailed processing logic?

For Logical Data Flow Diagram:

7   Are all physical aspects of the current system removed, unless constraints on the
         requirement?

8   Are any enquiries remaining after logicalisation major ones?

For Required System Data Flow Diagram:

9   Are all and only the facilities defined by the Selected Business System Option
         modelled in the Required System Data Flow Diagrams?

For the set:

10   Are appropriate flows at the lower level reflected at the higher level?

10   Are all identifiers unique?

11   Is the set of diagrams complete?

External Dependencies

Users closely involved with validation.

5.4   Data Flow Model

Purpose

To contain the overall information flow model of the system. This will be revised during the lifetime of the system to reflect Current Physical, Logical or Required System.

Suitability

Current Environment

A Physical Data Flow Model of the current environment is suitable where there is a current business situation that causes data to be transformed and where current work practices are structured and definable. It is also suitable where the scope of investigation is clear with defined external influences.

It is suitable where the:

- complexity of current business processes is high;
- stability of the environment is high;
- formality of current business processes is high;
- understanding of the existing system is high;
- quality of existing specifications is high.

Required system

The required system Data Flow Model is suitable for most situations as the start point for function and event identification. It is not necessary if the system to be built is only concerned with enquiries of the development of a database. Where the current system is being re-implemented to a large extent, the required Data Flow Model will be similar to or the same as the current logical DFM.

It is suitable where the:

- complexity of future business processes is high;
- formality of future business processes is high;
- availability, clarity and stability of requirements is high;
- complexity of computer system functions is high.

Composition

Data Flow Diagram – Level 1;

Data Flow Diagrams – Lower Level;

Elementary Process Descriptions;

External Entity Descriptions;

I/O Descriptions.

Position in System Development Template

Investigation.

Specification – External Design.

Quality Criteria:

1   Is the model variant identified and consistent for all components of the model?

2   Does the model accurately reflect the physical, logical or required system in terms of processes, external entities, data stores and data flows?

3   Is the model consistent with the previous version?

4   Are external entities, data stores and data flows represented consistently between levels?

5   Is there a consistent level of complexity between diagrams?

6   Are some processes decomposed into too many lower-level processes, suggesting the need for a further level of hierarchy?

7   Is this a complete set of documentation to fully describe the Data Flow Diagrams currently available (applies to current physical, logical and required system Data Flow Models)?

8   Have lower-level diagrams been created to represent detail of complex processes?

9   Is the set of diagrams complete?

10   Is there an adequate Elementary Process Description for all the bottom-level processes on the Data Flow Diagrams, including those that appear on the Level 1 diagram?

11   Has the description of common functionality been placed in Elementary Process Descriptions?

12   Are the common and other Elementary Process Descriptions cross-referenced consistently?

13   Are process identifiers and names consistent between the Data Flow Diagrams and the Elementary Process Descriptions?

14   Is there an adequate description of all the external entities identified within the Data Flow Model, including those that are decomposed and appear only on lower-level diagrams?

15   Are identifiers and names consistent within the model?

16   Are all bottom-level flows across the system boundary described?

17   Are only inputs and outputs crossing the system boundary described in I/O Descriptions?

18   Do the I/O Descriptions document all identified data flows which cross the system boundary?

Logical Data Flow Model:

19   Are all physical aspects of the current system removed, unless constraints on the requirement?

20   Are only major enquiries remaining after logicalisation?

External Dependencies

Users closely involved with validation.

5.5   Document Flow Diagram

Purpose

To model, as a graphical representation, the flow of documentation in a current system between external entities (sources and recipients). Several individual document flows may be drawn and then combined.

To assist in Data Flow Modelling, either to start or verify the analysis of data flows on the Current Physical Data Flow Model.

To assist in Business Activity Modelling.

Composition

Diagram elements represent:

- Documents;
- External entities;
- Data flows.

Position in System Development Template

Investigation.

Quality Criteria:

1   Are notational conventions adhered to?

2   Is the scope of the system clearly shown?

External Dependencies

Users closely involved with validation.

5.6   Elementary Process Description

Purpose

To record brief descriptions of the functionality of the following:

- Data Flow Model processes which are not the subject of decomposition to lower level Data Flow Diagrams;

- discrete elements of processing which are common to several bottom-level Data Flow Model processes (elementary processes).

Each instance of either of these is recorded as a separate Elementary Process Description, and these in their turn are packaged as a complete set.

These descriptions are used to support understanding of the Data Flow Model for use in later techniques.

Composition

Variant identifier, one of:

- Current Physical;

- Logical;

- Required System;

- Common.

Process identification (indicating if common or elementary process). (Note: common processing details are subsequently associated directly with the set of Function Definitions):

- Process identifier;

- Process name.

Common Processing cross-references (as appropriate)

Description of process.

Position in System Development Template

Investigation.

Specification – External Design.

Quality Criteria:

<u>For each</u>:

1   Is the variant identifier completed and valid?

2   Is the description of processing suitably detailed and appropriate to the Data Flow Modelling technique?

3   Is the common processing cross-reference (if used) valid?

4   Is the description consistent with any previous version?

5   Do the descriptions address issues in the Requirements Catalogue?

<u>Within Function Definitions</u>:

5   Are all the necessary descriptions of common processing linked with the Function Definitions?

<u>For the set</u>:

6   Are all elementary processes described?

External Dependencies

None.

5.7 External Entity Description

Purpose

All External Entity Descriptions associated with a Data Flow Model are packaged together to ensure that a complete set is compiled.

Each External Entity Description describes a real-world entity (whether another system, an Organisation, an individual or group of people) that interfaces to the system. It records any relevant detail about the responsibilities or functions of the external entity, and possible constraints on how it interfaces, or is required to interface, to the system.

To determine the match between user roles and the external entities on the Required System Data Flow Model.

Composition

Variant identifier, one of:

- Current Physical;

- Logical;

- Required System.

Multiple External Entity Descriptions each composed of:

- External entity identifier;

- External entity name;

- External entity description.

Position in System Development Template

Investigation.

Specification – External Design.

Quality Criteria:

For each:

1   Is the variant identifier completed and valid?

2   Is the external entity and its interaction with the system described sufficiently?

<u>For the set:</u>

3   Are all external entities described?

4   Is the set consistent with previous versions (modified as appropriate by Business
        System Options)?

External Dependencies

None

5.8   Function Definition

Purpose

To describe units of processing which need to be controlled as a whole in order to support users' tasks. Function Definitions have several purposes:

- to identify and define units of processing which need to be carried forward to physical design;

- to pull together products of analysis and design;

- to identify how to best organise the system processing to support the users' tasks which have been defined in Work Practice Modelling;

- to develop and confirm a common understanding between analyst and user of how the system processing is to be organised;

- to provide the basis for sizing and deriving design objectives.

Composition

Multiple function details each consisting of:

- Function Description;

- one or more I/O Structures.

Position in System Development Template

Specification – External Design.

Quality Criteria:

1   Is this a complete set of documentation for all identified functions?

2   Are the functions consistent with the description of tasks?

3   Are the functions logically defined with respect to identifying common function components?

4   Does each Function Definition which contains off-line processing have the appropriate I/O Structures, i.e., do the I/O Structures fully document input/output details for each function?

5   For functions containing on-line elements, do all UOM attributes appear in at least one Function Definition?

6   Is there at least one Function Definition for each required task which needs automated support?

External Dependencies

None.

5.9   Function Description

Purpose

To define a function which is to be provided by the required system to support a user's tasks. To provide a description of the function and cross-references to related products.

Suitability

Function Descriptions are suitable where the:

- size of the target domain is high;
- complexity of functions is high;
- formality of business processes is high.

Composition

Heading details:

- Function Name;
- Function Identifier;
- Function Type.

Function details:

- Function text;
- Potential Problems.

References to:

- Task or sub-task supported;
- Requirements Catalogue Entries;
- Related functions;
- DFD Processes;
- I/O Descriptions;
- I/O Structures;
- Event details, repeating group consisting of:

- ■ event name/ identifier;
- ■ event frequency.
  - • Enquiry details, repeating group consisting of:
    - ■ Enquiries;
    - ■ Enquiry Frequency.

Volumes.

Service Level Requirements, repeating group of:

- • Service Level Description;
- • Service Level Target Value;
- • Service Level Range;
- • Service Level Comments.

Position in System Development Template

Specification – External Design

Quality Criteria:

1   Is the Function Description complete in that all items that can be identified are present?

2   Is the function identifier unique?

3   If this is an on-line function, is it specified with cross-references to the User Object Model and Required Task Models?

4   If this is an off-line function, does it cross-reference the Required System Data Flow Model and I/O Structures?

5   Is the function classified according to all three types:

- ■ update or enquiry;
- ■ on-line or off-line;
- ■ user or system initiated?

External Dependencies

Relevant users to join the review team.

5.10 Input/Output (I/O) Descriptions

Purpose

To package all of the I/O Descriptions associated with a Data Flow Model to ensure that a complete set is compiled.

Each I/O Description entry records the data contained in one data flow that crosses the system boundary of a Data Flow Diagram (a data flow between an external entity and a process, in either direction).

The data items on the flows are listed; only bottom-level flows need be documented. Structure is not shown – neither repeating groups, nor optional items, nor choice of items. This lower level of detail will be rigorously defined during Function Definition. However, the practitioner may wish to record such detail as comments.

Composition

Variant identifier – one of:

- Current Physical;

- Logical;

- Required System.

I/O Descriptions, each consisting of:

- Source object identifier (from);

- Destination object identifier (to);

- Data flow name;

- Data content – including data item identifiers where appropriate;

- Comments.

Position in System Development Template

Specification – External Design

Quality Criteria:

For each:

1   Is the variant identifier completed correctly?

2   Is the list of data content complete from information available at this time?

3   Does the data flow include one or more data items?

For the set:

4   Are all input and output flows across the system boundary described?

5   Are only data flows which cross the system boundary described?

6   Is this set consistent with the previous version?

External Dependencies

Users will help to validate.

5.11 Input/Output (I/O) Structure

Purpose

To specify either the input or output data items for an off-line function (or function element), defining the sequencing within them.

Suitability

I/O Structures are most suitable where the input and output to functions has a pre-defined structure. They are less suitable where the structure of the I/O interface cannot be reasonably defined or controlled. They are not suitable for the definition of inputs and outputs which are on-line provided that the User Object Model and User Interface Design products are completed.

Composition

I/O Structure Diagram.

I/O Structure Element Description.

Position in System Development Template

Specification – External Design

Quality Criteria:

1   Are notational conventions (sequence, selection and iteration) used correctly on the I/O Structures?

2   Are all I/O Structure elements on the I/O Structure Diagram documented on the I/O Structure Element Description?

External Dependencies

Relevant users to join the review team.

5.12 Input/Output (I/O) Structure Diagram

Purpose

To show graphically the sequencing of data items or groups of data items within the data flows either into or out of an off-line function or off-line function component.

Composition

Identifier – function name and I/O Structure name.

Input/Output Type.

A diagrammatic representation of the function's inputs and outputs

Position in System Development Template

Specification – External Design.

Quality Criteria:

1   Is the function name correct and if there is more than one I/O Structure for the same function, is this I/O Structure uniquely identified?

2   Does the structure conform to the diagramming rules?

3   Are all I/O Structure Elements described in an I/O Structure Element Description?

External Dependencies

Relevant users to join the review team.

5.13 Input/Output (I/O) Structure Element Description

Purpose

To document the I/O Structures down to data item level. A central list of I/O Structure elements can be compiled to which individual I/O Structures refer.

Composition

Structure element details, is a repeating group of:

- I/O Structure element name;

- Data items associated with this element;

- Comments.

Position in System Development Template

Specification – External Design.

Quality Criteria:

1   Is the I/O Structure Element Description complete?

2   Does every I/O Structure element include at least one data item?

3   If the I/O Structure has been developed from one or more I/O Descriptions, does the I/O Structure Element Description contain all the relevant data items on those I/O Descriptions?

External Dependencies

Relevant users to join the review team.

5.14 Logical Data Store/Entity Cross-reference

Purpose

To document the correspondence of logically related groupings of entities from the Logical Data Model to main logical data stores derived during logicalisation of the Data Flow Diagrams. It is then used to identify the entities that are updated by events (found by inspection of Required System Data Flow Model). It should accurately reflect changes made in the transition from Logical Data Flow Model to Required System Logical Data Flow Model.

Composition

Each cross-reference details:

- logical data store identifier and name;
- entity names.

Position in System Development Template

Investigation.

Specification - External Design.

Quality Criteria:

1   Are all main logical data stores, derived during logicalisation of the Data Flow Diagrams, defined in terms of entities?

2   Is an entity in one and only one main logical data store?

3   Are all entities from the Logical Data Model mapped?

4   Does any logical data store appear more than once within the documentation? If so, why?

5   Where logically related groupings of entities are shown, is the structure consistent with the Logical Data Structure?

External Dependencies

User involvement in reviewing.

5.15 Logical/Physical Data Store Cross-reference

Purpose

To cross-reference main logical data stores to the physical data stores from the Current Physical Data Flow Model. It is created to aid the complete and consistent logicalisation of the Current Physical Data Flow Model, by listing logical data stores as they are derived. It is valuable as it ensures that no data held in the current system has been missed.

This product is an aid to logicalisation and is not maintained after the Logical Data Flow Model has been derived.

A data store from the current system may be referenced to more than one main logical data store, and one main logical data store may be referenced to more than one physical data store.

Composition

Logical data store details:

- identifier;
- name.

Physical data store details (may be for more than one):

- identifier;
- name.

Position in System Development Template

Investigation.

Specification – External Design.

Quality Criteria:

1   Have all physical data stores been mapped to a logical data store? That is, for each physical data store is there a logical data store containing the same entities?

2   Can physical data stores not appearing in the cross-reference be accounted for (for example, deleted as redundant)?

External Dependencies

None.

5.16 Process/Entity Matrix

Purpose

To aid identifying processes that access the same data, when deriving high-level groupings of processes at logicalisation. It is created with reference to the Logical Data Store/ Entity cross-reference, but not maintained after logicalisation.

This matrix is a guideline to help when logical groupings are not obvious. The intersections of the matrix show whether a given process updates a given entity (via a logical data store) or simply reads it, or does both or neither.

It is used to obtain groupings of bottom-level processes during the logicalisation of the Current Physical Data Flow Model.

Composition

Column headings: entity names.

Row headings: bottom-level process names.

Cells completed as appropriate.

Position in System Development Template

Specification – External Design.

Quality Criteria:

1   Are all of the entities from the Current Environment Logical Data Model used as column headings?

2   Are all of the bottom-level processes that exist after logicalisation used as row headings?

3   Are all data flows which access a main logical data store matched by a correct entry in the matrix?

4   Are all necessary cell values completed correctly? That is:

- 'u' (for 'update') when a process updates an entity;

- 'r' (for 'read') when there is a flow from the main logical data store to the process;

- null (an empty cell) denoting that the process does not access that entity.

External Dependencies

None.

5.17 Resource Flow Diagram

Purpose

To illustrate the movement of actual resources in the current services, rather than the information flows that document them. Resource flows and resource stores are reflected on the diagrams. Can be used as a start-up for Current Physical Data Flow Diagrams. Resource Flows and stores can be retained on the Current Physical Data Flow Model where no corresponding flow of information can be found.

Composition

Diagrammatic representation consisting of:

- process box;
- one or more external entities;
- resource flows between processes and other diagram elements;
- resource stores.

Position in System Development Template

Investigation.

Quality Criteria:

For each:

1   Are notational conventions adhered to?

2   Is the scope of the system clearly shown?

For the set:

3   Are all resources documented?

External Dependencies

Users closely involved with validation.

ANNEXE A – DESCRIPTION OF SYSTEM DEVELOPMENT TEMPLATE

The System Development Template (SDT) provides a common structure for the overall system development process. This template is used extensively in the definition of SSADM.

The System Development Template divides the development process into a number of distinct areas of concern, as shown in the diagram below.

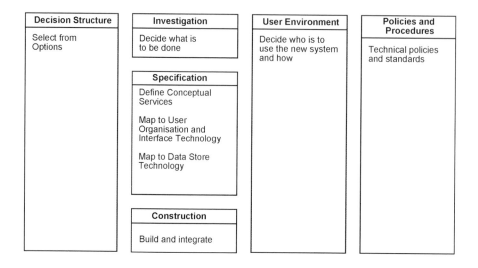

Figure A-1 System Development Template general view

The 3-schema specification architecture (which covers the Specification area) concentrates on those products that will ultimately lead, sometimes via other products, into elements of software. The SDT takes a broader view and divides the system development process into activity areas onto which all the development products may be mapped.

ANNEXE B – DESCRIPTION OF EU-RENT CASE STUDY

EU-Rent is a car rental company owned by EU-Corporation. It is one of three businesses – the other two being hotels and an airline – that each have their own business and IT systems, but share their customer base. Many of the car rental customers also fly with EU-Fly and stay at EU-Stay hotels.

EU-Rent business

EU-Rent has 1000 branches in towns all over Europe. At each branch cars, classified by car group, are available for rental. Each branch has a manager and booking clerks who handle rentals.

Rentals

Most rentals are by advance reservation; the rental period and the car group are specified at the time of reservation. EU-Rent will also accept immediate ('walk-in') rentals, if cars are available.

At the end of each day cars are assigned to reservations for the following day. If more cars have been requested than are available in a group at a branch, the branch manager may ask other branches if they have cars they can transfer to him/her.

Returns

Cars rented from one branch of EU-Rent may be returned to any other branch. The renting branch must ensure that the car has been returned to some branch at the end of the rental period. If a car is returned to a branch other than the one that rented it, ownership of the car is assigned to the new branch.

Servicing

EU-Rent also has service depots, each serving several branches. Cars may be booked for maintenance at any time provided that the service depot has capacity on the day in question.

For simplicity, only one booking per car per day is allowed. A rental or service may cover several days.

Customers

A customer can have several reservations but only one car rented at a time. EU-Rent keeps records of customers, their rentals and bad experiences such as late return, problems with payment and damage to cars. This information is used to decide whether to approve a rental.

Current IT system

Each branch and service depot has a local IT system based on PCs and a file server. The equipment is obsolete and limited in capacity (especially RAM). Hardware failures – screens, disk drives and power supplies – are increasingly frequent. There is currently no use of the Internet either for customer to business communication or for business to business communication.

Application maintainability

The application programs have been maintained over several years. Small RAM in the PCs has necessitated intricate, complex programs which makes amendments progressively more difficult and expensive.

Informal communication

Each location operates almost independently of others. Communication between locations is mainly by phone and fax and co-ordination is very variable. Sometimes, when a car is dropped off at a branch different from the pick-up branch, the drop-off branch will not inform the pick-up branch.

Branch managers tend to co-operate in small groups and not to look for 'spare' cars outside those groups. EU-Rent management feels that some capacity is wasted, but does not have reliable estimates of how much.

Scheduling of service bookings in branch and service depot files is co-ordinated by faxes between branch and depot. Sometimes service bookings are not recorded in the branch files, and cars booked for servicing are rented. Service depots sometimes do not get to know that a car has been transferred to a branch served by other depots until another depot requests the car's service history.

Customer blacklist

A copy of the customer blacklist is held at every branch. It should be updated every week from head office, but the logistics of updating the list with input from 1000 sources and sending out 1000 disks every week are beyond head office's capability. Updates are in fact sent out about every four weeks.

E-Commerce

There is no current use of e-commerce with customers having to phone or fax the individual offices to book cars for rental. This is causing problems in that some competitors have introduced facilities that enable customers to book and monitor their bookings over the Internet and it is thought that this is resulting in a loss of custom.

IT system replacement

EU-Rent management has decided that a new IT system is needed. It is expected whilst the basic operational activity is not expected to change significantly – locations and volume of rentals – it is expected that a number of 'online' systems (e.g. ordering of cars) will be implemented not necessarily as part of the initial role out but shortly thereafter. The new system is justified on three grounds:

- the current system cannot be kept going much longer;

- the perceived need to introduce some online system that can be accessed directly by customers over the Internet;

- better management of numbers of cars at branches and better co-ordination between branches is expected to increase utilisation of cars slightly – the same volume of business should be supportable with fewer cars. Each car ties up about 8,000 Euros in capital and loses about 3,000 Euros in depreciation, so significant savings are possible from small reductions in numbers of cars needed.

Corporate data

After the current IT system has been replaced, EU-Rent management wants to explore possibilities for sharing customer data across the car rental, hotel and airline systems. Even if customers are not stored in a single shared database, it makes sense for all three business areas to have consistent customer information on current address, telephone number, credit rating, etc.

It will be useful to know in each system when there are problems with a customer in other systems. And it may be possible to run promotions in one system, based on what EU-Corporation knows from the other systems about customers.

Future requirements

A customer loyalty incentive scheme is also under consideration. The requirement is not yet precisely defined but the scheme will be comparable with those offered by EU-Rent's competitors.

Members of the scheme will accumulate credit points with each car rental. They will exchange points for 'free' rentals. Only the base rental price will be payable by points; extra charges such as insurance and fuel will be paid for by cash or credit card. When this is introduced it is expected that customers will wish to be able to check (either by the use of a call-centre or directly over the Internet) the current state of their credit points.

Rationale for EU-Rent

The business of EU-Rent is car rentals, but this is largely irrelevant; it merely provides an easily understood context for examples. The business issues and user requirements in EU-Rent could be easily mapped to other systems. They include:

- a requirement to deliver a range of services (rental of cars of different quality and price) at many locations (rental branches), with different volumes of business and patterns of demand;

- customers who may use more than one location, but whose business with the whole organisation should be tracked;

- strong general policies set centrally (car models that may be used, rental tariffs, procedures for dealing with customers), but significant flexibility and authority for local managers (number of cars owned by branch, authority to over-ride published tariff to beat competitors' prices);

- a requirement for customers to be able to directly access aspects of the system;

- performance targets for local managers;

- a requirement for capacity planning and resource replenishment (disposal and purchase of cars, moving of cars between branches); possibilities for this to be managed locally, regionally or centrally;

- locally-managed sharing or swapping of resources or customers between branches to meet short-term unforeseen demand;

- an internal support structure (the maintenance depots) needed to maintain the resources and ensure that the product delivered to customers is of adequate quality;

- a customer base that is shared with other, separate systems (EU-Stay hotels and EU-Fly airline), and possibilities of communicating or co-ordinating with these systems.

Many of these characteristics are common to other types of business; for example, health care, vocational training, social security, policing, retail chain stores, branch banking.

ANNEXE C – GLOSSARY OF TERMS

Business System Options

The set of Business System Options which is compiled so that a selection can be made. The selected Business System Option is a description of a chosen system development direction. The description documents the system boundary, inputs, outputs and the transformation taking place within the boundary. Essentially the description is textual with supporting products such as Data Flow Diagrams.

Context Diagram

A Data Flow Diagram consisting of a single process to represent the system and external entities to which information is given or information is received by the system. This may be drawn to illustrate the initial scope of the proposed system. The diagram concentrates on the major inputs and outputs of the system and shows the external sources and recipients of system data.

Current Physical Data Flow Model

Shows how the current services are organised and processing is undertaken. An overview of current services is provided by documenting only the Level 1 Data Flow Diagram.

data flow

Shows where data is being passed between different elements on a Data Flow Diagram. The name associated with the data flow should be meaningful to those reviewing the Data Flow Diagram.

Data flows will pass into and out of the system and between processes (generally via data stores except on the Current Physical Data Flow Model where process-to-process flows may reflect inadequacies in the current system). When the system boundary is being defined there may even be data flows between external entities.

At the lowest level of the Data Flow Diagram these are 'simple' data flows, though they may be combined into 'composite data flows' on higher level diagrams.

A data flow can be regarded as the data content of potential flows of data between elements of a Data Flow Diagram. Elementary data flows between elements on the bottom level diagrams may be aggregated in summary-level Data Flow Diagrams to form a hierarchy of data flows consistent with the hierarchy of DFD processes.

Data Flow Diagram (DFD)

A diagram representing the flow of information around a system, the way in which it is changed and stored and the sources and recipients of data outside the boundary of the system. Each Data Flow Diagram contains processes, data stores, external entities and data flows.

Data Flow Model (DFM)

A set of Data Flow Diagrams and their associated documentation. The diagrams form a hierarchy with the Data Flow Diagram Level 1 showing the scope of the system and the lower level diagrams expanding the detail as appropriate. Additional documentation provides a description of the processes, input/output data flows and external entities.

Data Flow Modelling

Is used to help define the scope of the system and ensure that the analysts have a clear understanding of the user's problems and requirements.

The technique is used to build a model of the information flows and not to define the detail of the processing performed by the system.

data item

Any element of data that is used within the system. Each data item may fulfil a number of different roles, each of which will be constrained by this central definition.

data store

A collection of any type of data in any form as represented on a Data Flow Diagram. In the Current Physical Data Flow Model, this may be a computer file or a box of documents or any other means of storing data.

Each data store is of one of the following types:

- **Main**. A repository of data which persists for a period of time. In the Logical and Required System Data Flow Models, a main data store represents a portion of the Logical Data Model. Each main data store must be composed of one or more entities;

- **Transient**. A type of data store which is temporary, accumulating data for use by another process when it is subsequently deleted. This data is not described within the Conceptual Model.

Document Flow Diagram

Shows how documents pass around the system. This may be the initial diagram drawn within the Data Flow Modelling technique to assist in defining/identifying the boundary of the system. This diagram will be produced if the current system is predominantly clerical and involves the passing of information using forms or other documents.

Elementary Process Description

Each process at the lowest level of decomposition (i.e., which is indicated by an asterisk as being at the bottom level) is described by an Elementary Process Description (EPD).

An Elementary Process Description is a brief textual description of the process. This description may contain the following:

- what data is accessed;

- what business constraints dictate how the process is carried out;

- circumstances under which the process is invoked;

- constraints on when and by whom the process can be invoked.

entity

Something, whether concrete or abstract, which is of relevance to the system and about which information needs to be stored.

external entity

Whatever or whoever donates data to or receives data from the system. Represented on Data Flow Diagrams as an oval. An external entity may be another system, an external file/database, an organisation, an individual or a group of people.

External Entity Description

Used to explain, briefly, the relevance of an external entity in relation to the existing or proposed system. The detail will cover responsibilities or functions of the external entity and any constraints on the interface with the proposed system.

function

A user-defined packaging of events and enquiries and the processing they trigger that will be accessed from the External Design. Functions can be categorised as on-line (contain some element of user interaction) or off-line (contain no element of user interaction).

Function Definition (technique)

Function Definition identifies units of processing specification, or functions, which package together the essential services of the system in the way required by the user organisation.

Function Definition (product)

The product of the Function Definition technique is a group products called the Function Definition. This is composed of the following products:

- Function Description;

- I/O Structure.

Function Description

The Function Description contains some descriptive text and a large number of cross-references to other products. The precise format of the product will depend upon the documentation tools available to the project.

I/O Descriptions

Are used to document all data flows which cross the Data Flow Model system boundary. They list the data items contained in the data flows. Detail of the structure of the data – such as repeating groups and optionality – need not be included, since this will be rigorously defined on I/O Structures.

I/O Structure

Structure diagram representing data input to and output from functions. An I/O Structure consists of an I/O Structure Diagram optionally supported by an I/O Structure Element Description. I/O Structures are produced for each function:

- I/O Structure Diagrams are a pictorial representation of the data items which are input to a function and output from a function;

- I/O Structure Element Descriptions are the backing documentation for the I/O Structure Diagram and list the data items represented by each element of the I/O Structure Diagram.

Logical Data Flow Model

A variant of Data Flow Model.

A logical model of the current services, free of physical or organisational constraints. The Logical Data Flow Model is created from the Current Physical Data Flow Model, by carrying out specific activities. The aim is to remove duplication in processing and data stores, and to re-group bottom-level processes into the functional areas that the user requires.

Logical Data Store/Entity Cross-reference

Is a product showing the correspondence between logical data stores in the Logical or Required System Data Flow Model and the entities on the Logical Data Model. This is used to ensure that a main data store corresponds to an entity or group of entities. Also each entity on the Logical Data Model must be held completely within one and only one main data store on the Logical or Required System Data Flow Model. (Transient data stores are not included in the Logical Data Store/Entity Cross-reference)

off-line function

A function where all the data is input and the whole of the database processing for the function is completed without further interaction with the user.

on-line function

A function where the system and the user communicate through input and output messages, i.e., message pairs. The system responds in time to influence the next input message. On-line functions may include off-line elements such as printing an off-line report.

process

Transforms or manipulates information (data) in a system. Appears within a Data Flow Model. Can be hierarchically decomposed.

Required System Data Flow Model

A variant of the Data Flow Model which represents the new system without any physical constraints but structured around the user's view of the system. The Required System Data Flow Model is based on one of the following:

- the Logical Data Flow Model, tailored to meet the scope of the Selected Business System Option and to satisfy the requirements recorded in the Requirements Catalogue;

- the Data Flow Diagram which supports the selected Business System Option;

- the Business Activity Model which identifies the essential activities that must be performed in support of the new system.

System Development Template

The System Development Template provides a common structure for the overall system development process.

It divides the process into a number of distinct areas of concern:

- Investigation;

- Specification;

- Construction;

- Decision Structure;

- User Organisation;

- Policies and Procedures.

The Specification area contains the Three-schema Specification Architecture which is made up of the areas Conceptual Model, Internal Design and External Design. The Three-schema Specification Architecture concentrates on those products that will ultimately lead, sometimes via other products, into elements of software. The System Development Template takes a broader view. It divides the system development process into activity areas onto which the development products may be mapped.

transient data store

Transient data is held for a short time before being used by a process and then deleted. Data held in transient data stores may not be structured in the same way as the data in a main data store.

INDEX

T

U

V

W